W9-COX-244

THE NEW
PAINT EFFECTS
PROJECT BOOK

THE NEW
PAINT EFFECTS
PROJECT BOOK

Learn 100 decorative painting techniques, with practical
examples and step-by-step projects to transform your home

SACHA COHEN AND MAGGIE PHILO

HERMES
HOUSE

This edition is published by Hermes House

Hermes House is an imprint of
Anness Publishing Ltd
Hermes House
88–89 Blackfriars Road
London SE1 8HA
tel. 020 7401 2077
fax 020 7633 9499
info@anness.com

© Anness Publishing Ltd 2004

All rights reserved. No part of this publication may be reproduced, stored in a retrieval
system, or transmitted in any way or by any means, electronic, mechanical, photocopying,
recording or otherwise, without the prior written permission of the copyright holder.

A CIP catalogue record for this book
is available from the British Library.

Publisher: Joanna Lorenz
Editorial Director: Judith Simons
Project Editor: Felicity Forster
Copy Editor: Judy Cox
Photographers: Lizzie Orme and Adrian Taylor
Project Contributors: Petra Boase, Sacha Cohen, Lucinda Ganderton,
Elaine Green, Emma Hardy and Liz Wagstaff
Stylists: Katie Gibbs and Judy Williams
Designer: Bill Mason
Editorial Reader: Jay Thundercliffe
Production Controller: Steve Lang

Previously published as *Complete Paint Effects*

1 3 5 7 9 10 8 6 4 2

CONTENTS

INTRODUCTION

Home decorating is not simply a matter of painting your walls with white emulsion (latex); there is a wealth of different paints in amazing colours, and many original, easy ways to apply them, both to walls and to the objects within the room itself. With just a little imagination and a lot of fun, you can create originality and colour throughout your home. This book brings together the easiest and most adaptable of decorative paint techniques, together with fabulous ideas for applying them to the surfaces of your home. The projects range from the simple to the more complicated, so there is something for every level of expertise and ability. Each project is explained fully with clear step-by-step instructions and photographs. If you are planning to overhaul a whole room, you will find many ideas for different ways of decorating walls, doors, even floors. Why not create instant limewashed walls, antique-effect doors or stunning imitation kitchen tiles? Alternatively, you can use stencils and stamping to add a distinctive pattern of Greek urns, animal friezes or celestial cherubs to a wall. Decorating smaller objects – such as picture frames, trays, candles and cushions – will also add interest to plain surfaces. Each of the main sections on paint effects, stencilling and stamping is preceded by invaluable advice on all the basic techniques for that effect as well as details of the materials and equipment that you will need. There is also clear guidance on mixing your own paint, working with glazes and varnishes, and making your own stencils and stamps. Armed with this compendium of decorative projects, you will never be short of inspiration.

PAINT EFFECTS

Many people find the thought of painting their homes rather daunting, but a room can be completely transformed by just a single layer of well-chosen paint. If you use some of the decorative paint effects described in this first section of the book, such as trompe l'oeil three-dimensional panels, frescoes, crackle glazing, sponging and graining, the room is guaranteed to look unusual, stylish and highly professional. Today, there is an ever-increasing range of beautiful paints to choose from as well as helpful facilities in many shops for mixing your own paints to create a highly individual scheme. You may find yourself getting carried away with colour!

ABOVE: Distress a piece of furniture by rubbing back thin layers of paint. Decorate with a simple handpainted leaf design.

LEFT: This textured paint effect is achieved by pressing tissue paper over the wet surface.

PAINTING MATERIALS

Acrylic or emulsion (latex) paint and acrylic scumble glaze are the main painting materials that you will need to put a wide variety of paint techniques into practice.

Acrylic primer is a quick-drying water-based primer. It is used to prime new wood.

Acrylic scumble is a slow-drying, water-based medium with a milky, gel-like appearance, which dries clear. It adds texture and translucency to the paint, and the marks you make with brushes, sponges and other tools are held in the glaze.

Acrylic varnish is available in a satin or matt (flat) finish. It is used to seal paint effects to give a more durable and protective finish to the surface. Acrylic floor varnish is extremely hardwearing and should be used on floors.

Artist's acrylic paint can be found in art and craft shops and comes in a wide range of colours. It gives various paint effects a subtle translucent quality.

Crackle glaze is brushed on to a surface, causing the paint laid over it to crack in random patterns to create an aged appearance.

Emulsion paint is opaque and comes in a choice of matt (flat) or satin finish. Satin finish is best for the base colour and matt for paint effects. Use sample pots of paint if you need only a small amount.

Methylated spirits (methyl alcohol) is a solvent that will dissolve emulsion (latex) paint and can therefore be used to distress paint. It is also used as a solvent, thinner and brush cleaner for shellac.

Pure powder pigment can be used to colour paint and can be mixed with acrylic scumble, clear wax or emulsion (latex) paint. It is also used for vinegar graining.

Shellac is a type of varnish, which is available in clear and brown shades. French polish and button polish are in fact shellac and may be easier to find. Shellac can be used to seal wood, metal leaf and paint.

Wax is available in neutral and in brown. It will seal and colour paint. Neutral wax can be mixed with powder pigment.

RIGHT: 1 powder pigments, 2 emulsion (latex) paints, 3 acrylic primer, 4 artist's acrylic paint, 5 acrylic scumble, 6 crackle glaze, 7 neutral wax, 8 brown wax, 9 methylated spirits (methyl alcohol), 10 brown shellac, 11 clear shellac.

PAINTING EQUIPMENT

Different paint effects require different tools. Most of the tools illustrated are cheap and they are easily found in do-it-yourself or decorating suppliers.

Abrasives include abrasive paper and wire (steel) wool, which come in many grades. They are used for distressing paint.

Artist's paintbrushes are needed to paint fine detail.

Decorator's paintbrushes are used to apply emulsion (latex) paint, washes and glazes. They come in a wide range of sizes.

Flat varnish brushes can be used for painting and varnishing. They are often the choice of the experts.

Masking tape comes in many types. Easy-mask and low-tack tapes are less likely to pull off paintwork, and flexible tape is good for going around curves. Fine line tape is useful for creating a narrow negative line.

Measuring equipment such as a ruler, spirit level, set square (T square) and plumbline are needed to mark out designs.

Mutton cloth is very absorbent and can be used for paint effects. Cotton cloths are also used for ragging and polishing.

Natural sponges are used for sponging. They are valued for their textural quality. Synthetic sponges can be used for colourwashing.

Paint containers such as paint kettles, trays and pots are used to mix and store paint.

Paint rollers, small and large, are used to provide an even-textured base colour without brushmarks. They are also used to create textured paint effects.

Rubber combs and heart grainers are used to create textured patterns in paint glazes. Heart grainers (rockers) create an effect of the heart grain of wood.

Softening brushes are used for blending colours together.

Stencil brushes are for stippling paint on to smaller surfaces.

Stippling brushes are usually rectangular, and are used to even out the texture of glaze and to avoid brushmarks.

RIGHT: 1 paint containers, 2 spirit level, 3 plumbline, 4 kitchen paper, 5 artist's brushes, 6 decorator's brushes, 7 flat varnish brushes, 8 hog softening brush, 9 stencil brush, 10 paint rollers, 11 gloves, 12 stippling brush, 13 masking tapes, 14 measuring equipment, 15 craft knife and pencil, 16 heart grainer (rocker), 17 combs, 18 natural and synthetic sponges, 19 mutton cloth (stockinet), 20 rag, 21 wire (steel) wool and abrasive paper.

PAINTING TECHNIQUES

Most of the projects in this chapter are based on a few simple techniques. These can be used on their own, or combined to produce an infinite variety of paint effects. The techniques shown here all use ultramarine blue emulsion (latex) paint. This has been mixed with acrylic scumble glaze and/or water, as appropriate, to achieve the desired effect. Two coats of satin finish white emulsion paint were rollered on as a base. This provides an even-textured, non-absorbent finish, which is ideal to work on as it allows glazes to dry more slowly and evenly than emulsion paint. It also means that if you make any mistakes they are easily wiped off. All these techniques, except the crackle glaze, can be done with artist's acrylic paint mixed with scumble, in which case the effects will look more translucent.

Sponging

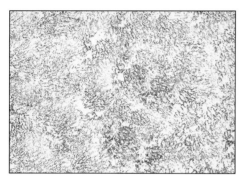

Dilute a little paint with a little water in a paint tray or on a saucer. Dip a damp natural sponge into the paint and wipe off the excess on kitchen paper. Dab the sponge evenly on to the prepared surface in different directions.

Sponging and dispersion

Follow the technique as for sponging, then rinse the sponge in clean water and dab it over the sponged paint before it dries to soften the effect.

Combing

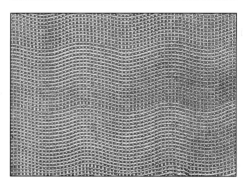

Mix the paint with acrylic scumble and brush on with cross-hatched brushstrokes. Run a metal or rubber graining comb through the wet glaze to make a pattern. This pattern was done with straight vertical strokes followed by wavy horizontal ones.

Colourwashing

Dilute the paint with water and brush on randomly with cross-hatched brushstrokes, using a large decorator's brush. Alternatively, a damp sponge will give a similar effect.

Rubbing in colourwash

Dilute the paint with water and brush on. Use a clean cotton rag to disperse the paint. Alternatively, apply it directly with the rag and rub in.

Frottage

Apply paint with cross-hatched brushstrokes, then press a piece of tissue paper over the wet surface and peel it off. The paint can be diluted with water or scumble.

Dabbing with a mutton cloth

Brush on paint mixed with scumble, using cross-hatched brushstrokes. Dab a mutton cloth (stockinet) over the wet glaze to even out the texture and eliminate the brushstrokes.

Ragging

Mix paint with scumble and brush on, using cross-hatched brushstrokes. Scrunch up a piece of cotton rag and dab this on the wet paint in all directions, twisting your hand for a random look. When the rag becomes too paint-soaked, use a new one.

Rag rolling without brushmarks

Brush on paint mixed with scumble and dab with a mutton cloth (stockinet) to eliminate brushmarks. Scrunch a cotton rag into a sausage shape and roll over the surface, changing direction as you go. Use a new piece of rag when it becomes too wet.

Stippling

Brush on paint mixed with acrylic scumble, using cross-hatched brushstrokes. Pounce a stippling brush over the wet glaze, working from the bottom upwards to eliminate brushmarks and provide an even-textured surface. Keep the brush as dry as possible by regularly wiping the bristles with kitchen paper.

Dragging

Mix paint with scumble glaze and brush on with cross-hatched brushstrokes. Drag a flat decorator's brush through the wet glaze, keeping a steady hand. The soft effect shown here is achieved by going over the wet glaze a second time to break up the vertical lines.

Crackle glaze

Brush on a coat of water-based crackle glaze and leave to dry according to the manufacturer's instructions. Using a well-laden brush, apply paint carefully on top so that you lay, rather than brush, it over the surface. Work quickly and do not overbrush an area already painted. If you have missed an area, touch it in when the paint has dried. Seal with acrylic varnish.

MIXING PAINTS AND GLAZES

There are no precise recipes for mixing glazes and washes. Generally, the proportion of emulsion (latex) paint to scumble is 1 part paint to 6 parts scumble. This will give soft, semi-translucent colour that is suitable for effects such as ragging, dragging and combing where you want the coloured glaze to hold the marks you have made. You can reduce the amount of scumble if you want a more opaque coverage. However the paint will dry more quickly so it may be harder to maintain a wet edge for an even result. When you are mixing scumble with artist's acrylic paint, the amount of paint you should use depends on the depth of colour you need. Acrylic paint mixed with scumble gives a more translucent colour. It is used in exactly the same way as the emulsion glazes and washes.

If you do not need the texture provided by the scumble (for example, when colourwashing) but you want to dilute the colour, use water. This is cheaper but it dries more quickly, which may be a disadvantage. If you want to slow down the drying time, add a 50/50 mix of water and scumble to the paint. Emulsion paint can be diluted with any amount of water, and several thin washes of colour will give a more even cover than one thick wash.

Try to mix up enough colour to complete the area you are to decorate. Washes and glazes stretch a long way, but if in doubt, mix up more than you think you might need. If you want to repeat the effect, measure the quantities you use. Before you start, painting samples on to scrap wood will give you the truest effect.

Ragging with acrylic paint and scumble.

Ragging with emulsion (latex) paint and scumble.

Colourwashing with one wash of equal parts emulsion (latex) paint and water.

Colourwashing with four thin washes of 1 part paint to 8 parts water to achieve the same colour saturation.

WORKING WITH COLOUR

Paint effects can vary widely according to your choice of colour and the way in which you use it. Whether you put a light colour over a dark base or a dark colour over a light one is a matter of choice, although a translucent pale colour would not really be visible over a dark base. A bright base colour can give added depth and a subtle glow beneath a dark top coat, while using the colours the other way round will tone down a bright colour. Tone-on-tone colour combinations are good for a subtle effect and are always a safe bet, but experiment with contrasting colours for exciting results.

Many of the techniques in this section use layers of several different colours. Greater depth and texture are achieved when you build up colours in this way, but a simple technique with one colour can be just as effective. It depends on the look you want and the furnishings in the room.

If you want to tone down a paint effect, you can lighten it by brushing over a wash of very diluted white or off-white emulsion (latex) paint. You can also tone down a colour by darkening it. A wash of raw umber paint works well over most colours and has a much warmer feel than black.

Adding white to lighten bright blue colourwashing.

Adding raw umber to darken bright red colourwashing.

Sponging – light yellow over deep yellow (left), deep yellow over light yellow (right).

Dabbing with a mutton cloth (stockinet) – dull green over emerald green (left), emerald green over dull green (right).

Frottage – tone-on-tone, deep blue over light blue (left), two tones of contrasting colours, bright blue over orange (right).

Colourwashing (left) in orange, red and crimson, finishing with the darkest colour on the top surface. Layers of sponging (right) in three shades of blue-green, finishing with the lightest colour on the top surface.

MIXING COLOURS

Emulsion (latex) paint is available in a huge range of ready-mixed colours. If you use acrylic paint or pure powder pigment you will need to mix your own colours.

Most colours can be mixed from yellow, cyan blue, magenta, black and white, but a basic palette of 14 colours plus black and white will allow you to mix an enormous range of colours. The suggested palette consists of yellow ochre, cadmium yellow, raw sienna, burnt sienna, red ochre, cadmium red, alizarin crimson, ultramarine blue, Prussian blue, cerulean blue, viridian green, oxide of chromium, raw umber and burnt umber. These basic colours are beautiful alone, and many other colours can be made by mixing them.

Some colour combinations are unexpected, and there are no hard-and-fast rules about which colours should or should not be mixed. If you experiment, you will soon develop confidence and a good eye for mixing colour.

Yellows and browns (right)

1 Cadmium yellow and white

2 Cadmium yellow

3 Cadmium yellow and
*   viridian green*

4 Yellow ochre and white

5 Yellow ochre

6 Raw sienna

7 Burnt sienna

8 Burnt umber

9 Raw umber

Reds

Yellows and browns

Reds (opposite)

1 *Alizarin crimson, cadmium yellow and white*
2 *Cadmium red and cadmium yellow*
3 *Red ochre*
4 *Red ochre and white*
5 *Cadmium red and burnt umber*
6 *Cadmium red*
7 *Cadmium red and black*
8 *Alizarin crimson*
9 *Alizarin crimson and oxide of chromium*

Blues (top right)

1 *Cerulean blue, raw umber and white*
2 *Prussian blue, black and white*
3 *Prussian blue*
4 *Cerulean blue*
5 *Ultramarine blue and white*
6 *Ultramarine blue*
7 *Alizarin crimson, ultramarine blue and white*
8 *Alizarin crimson and ultramarine blue*
9 *Ultramarine blue and raw umber*

Greens (right)

1 *Prussian blue and yellow ochre*
2 *Prussian blue and cadmium yellow*
3 *Prussian blue, cadmium yellow and white*
4 *Ultramarine and yellow ochre*
5 *Oxide of chromium*
6 *Viridian green and cadmium yellow*
7 *Viridian green*
8 *Viridian green, raw umber and white*
9 *Prussian blue, yellow ochre and white*

Blues

Greens

ROUGH PLASTER COLOURWASH

This sunny yellow wall was given a rough-textured look by trowelling on a ready-mixed medium (joint compound), available from do-it-yourself stores, which is normally used for smoothing walls and ceilings that have unwanted texture. Colourwashing in two shades of yellow gives added depth and tone. The absorbent wall surface picks up varying degrees of paint, and there will be some areas which are not coloured at all, but this is all part of the attractive rural effect.

You will need

- medium (joint compound) for coating walls
- plasterer's trowel or large scraper
- large decorator's paintbrush
- emulsion (latex) paint in white
- emulsion (latex) paint, in two different shades of bright yellow
- household sponge

1 Apply the coating medium (joint compound) to the wall, using a plasterer's trowel or large scraper. You can decide whether to have a very rough effect or a smoother finish. Leave to dry overnight.

2 Using a large decorator's paintbrush, paint the wall with two coats of white emulsion (latex), leaving each coat of paint to dry thoroughly.

3 Dilute one shade of yellow paint with about 75 per cent water. Dip a damp sponge into the paint and wipe it over the wall, using plenty of arm movement as though you were cleaning it.

4 Leave the first shade of yellow paint to dry. Dilute the second shade of yellow paint with about 75 per cent water and wipe it over the first colour in the same way.

DIAMOND-STENCILLED WALL

Here a stunning colour scheme is created by dragging a deep green glaze over a lime green base. The surface is then stencilled with shiny aluminium leaf diamonds, which stand out against the strong background. This paint finish would look very dramatic in a dining room, with muted lighting used to catch the metallic diamond highlights.

You will need

- 2 large decorator's paintbrushes
- emulsion (latex) paint in lime green
- artist's acrylic paint in monestial green and emerald green
- acrylic scumble
- pencil
- stencil card (stock)
- craft knife
- cutting mat or thick card (stock)
- 2 artist's paintbrushes
- acrylic size
- aluminium leaf
- make-up brush
- clear shellac and brush

1 Using one of the large decorator's brushes, paint the wall with lime green emulsion (latex) paint. Leave to dry.

2 Mix a glaze from 1 part monestial green acrylic paint, 1 part emerald green acrylic paint and 6 parts acrylic scumble. Paint the glaze on to the wall with random brushstrokes.

3 Working quickly with a dry large decorator's brush, go over the surface using long, downward strokes. Overlap the strokes and don't stop mid-stroke. Leave to dry.

4 Draw a small diamond shape in pencil on to stencil card (stock). Cut out the shape, using a craft knife and cutting mat or thick card.

5 Using an artist's paintbrush, apply a thin, even coat of acrylic size through the stencil card on to the wall. Repeat the diamond motif as many times as desired to make a decorative pattern.

6 After about 20 minutes, touch the size lightly with a finger to check that it has become tacky. If not, wait a little longer. Press a piece of aluminium leaf gently on to the size.

7 Working carefully, peel off the aluminium leaf, then brush off the excess with the make-up brush.

8 Using the second artist's paintbrush, apply clear shellac over the diamond motifs. Leave to dry.

LIMEWASHED WALL

For an instant limewashed effect, apply white emulsion (latex) paint over a darker base with a dry brush, then remove some of the paint with a cloth soaked in methylated spirits (methyl alcohol). This is a good way to decorate uneven or damaged walls, and gives a pleasing rustic effect.

You will need

- matt emulsion (flat latex) paint in cream and white
- 2 large decorator's paintbrushes
- clean cotton cloths
- methylated spirits (methyl alcohol)
- neutral wax

1 Paint the wall with a coat of cream matt emulsion (flat latex) paint, using one of the large decorator's brushes. Leave to dry.

2 Using the second decorator's brush, dip the tip of the dry paintbrush into the white emulsion paint. Using random strokes, dry brush the paint on to the wall. Leave to dry.

3 Using a cloth, rub methylated
spirits (methyl alcohol) into the wall
in some areas. This will remove some of
the paint, giving a natural weathered
effect. Leave to dry.

4 Using a clean cloth, rub wax all
over the wall to seal the paint and
protect the surface.

FRESCO EFFECT

A dry brush and cloth are used here to soften rough brushstrokes and give the faded effect of Italian fresco painting. This wall treatment is the ideal background for a mural, so if you are feeling artistic you could paint a scene on top.

You will need

- emulsion (latex) paint in pale pink and ultramarine
- acrylic scumble
- 2 large decorator's paintbrushes
- clean cotton cloth

1 Begin by mixing a glaze of 1 part pale pink emulsion (latex) paint to 6 parts acrylic scumble. Paint the glaze on to the top half of the wall with random brushstrokes.

2 Using a dry brush, go over the top half of the wall while the glaze is still wet to even out the brushstrokes.

3 Rub a clean cotton cloth into the glaze with circular motions, to produce the faded effect of Italian fresco painting.

4 Repeat steps 1–3 on the bottom half of the wall, using ultramarine paint. Softly blend the two colours together with a dry brush.

MISTY LILAC STRIPES

Here, wide stripes are painted and the wet paint dabbed with mutton cloth (stockinet) to soften the effect and blend in brushmarks. As an extra touch, paint a triangle at the top of each stripe. If you do not have a picture rail, take the stripes up to the top of the wall and place the triangles along the skirting (base) board.

You will need

- satin-finish emulsion (latex) paint in white
- paint roller and tray
- ruler and pencil
- plumbline
- masking tape
- emulsion (latex) paint in lilac
- acrylic scumble
- medium decorator's paintbrush
- mutton cloth (stockinet)
- small piece of card (stock)
- scissors
- paint guard or strip of card (stock)

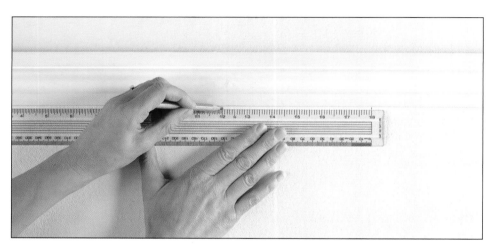

1 Paint the walls with white satin-finish emulsion (latex) paint, using a paint roller and tray. Mark the centre of the most important wall, below the picture rail (if you have one), with a pencil. Make marks 7.5cm/3in either side of this, then every 15cm/6in. Continue making 15cm/6in marks around the room until the marks meet at the least noticeable corner.

2 Hang a short length of plumbline from one of the marks, and mark with a dot where it rests. Hang the plumbline from this dot and mark where it rests. Continue down the wall. Repeat for each mark below the picture rail.

3 Starting in the centre of the wall, place strips of masking tape either side of the marked row of dots to give a 15cm/6in wide stripe. Repeat for the other rows of dots.

4 Dilute some of the lilac paint with about 25 per cent water and 25 per cent acrylic scumble. Brush on to a section of the first stripe. Complete each stripe in two or three stages, depending on the height of the room, blending the joins to get an even result.

5 Dab the wet paint lightly with a mutton cloth (stockinet) to smooth out the brushmarks. Complete all the stripes, then carefully peel away the masking tape and leave the paint to dry.

6 Cut a card (stock) triangle with a 15cm/6in base and measuring 10cm/4in from the base to the tip. Use this as a template to mark the centre of each of the stripes, lilac and white, 10cm/4in below the picture rail.

7 Working on one stripe at a time, place strips of masking tape between the top corners of the stripe and the marked dot, as shown.

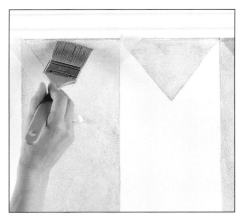

8 Brush on the lilac paint mix, then dab the mutton cloth over the wet paint as before. Leave the paint to dry. Repeat for all the stripes.

9 Dilute some lilac paint with about 20 parts water. Brush over the wall in all directions to give a hint of colour to the white stripes.

10 Add a little paint to the remaining diluted mixture to strengthen the colour. Using a paint guard or strip of card to protect the painted wall, brush the paint on to the picture rail.

RED-PANELLED WALL

This bright red wall has been beautifully toned down with a translucent glaze of deep maroon acrylic paint mixed with scumble. The panel has been given a very simple trompe l'oeil treatment, using dark and light shades of paint to create a 3-D effect.

You will need

- satin-finish emulsion (latex) paint in bright red
- medium and small decorator's paintbrushes
- ruler and pencil
- spirit level
- plumbline
- masking tape
- craft knife
- artist's acrylic paint in deep maroon, black and white
- acrylic scumble
- mutton cloth (stockinet)
- clean cotton cloth
- coarse-grade abrasive paper

1 Paint the wall with two coats of bright red paint, leaving each coat to dry. Mark the centre top of the panel. Draw a horizontal line 30cm/12in either side of this mark.

2 Drop a plumbline 90cm/36in down from each end of the drawn line and make a mark. Draw a line between all the marked points to give a 60 × 90cm/24 × 36in panel.

3 Place strips of masking tape around the outer edge of the panel. Neaten the corners where the strips of tape meet with a craft knife.

4 Mix the maroon paint with acrylic scumble to the required colour. Brush this on to the panel.

5 Immediately dab a mutton cloth (stockinet) over the wet glaze to even out the texture. Leave the glaze to dry.

6 Starting in a corner, brush the maroon glaze on to a section of the wall, roughly the same size as the panel. Dab it with the mutton cloth to blend the brushmarks as before, stopping just short of the edge of the panel. Roll up the cotton cloth into a sausage shape and then immediately roll it over the wet glaze, changing direction to give a more random effect. Leave the glaze to dry. Repeat all over the rest of the wall.

7 Remove the masking tape. Place new strips of tape either side of the bright red line now revealed and trim the corners with the craft knife. Mix a small amount of black acrylic paint with some of the maroon glaze. Brush this between the masking tape down one side of the panel, on the side where the light source is. Place a piece of coarse-grade abrasive paper diagonally at the top and clean off the glaze that extends beyond. Keeping the abrasive paper in the same position, repeat on the top border of the panel.

8 Add a small amount of white acrylic paint to the maroon glaze and apply to the remaining two borders in the same way. Leave to dry, then carefully remove the masking tape.

TWO-TONE ROLLERED WALL

For this quick, ingenious paint effect, two shades of emulsion (latex) are placed next to each other in a paint tray and then rollered on to the wall together. Moving the roller in different directions blends the paint very effectively.

You will need

◆ paint roller and tray
◆ emulsion (latex) paint in cream, yellow and terracotta

1 Using a paint roller, paint the wall with a base coat of cream emulsion (latex). Leave to dry.

2 Pour the yellow and the terracotta emulsion into the paint tray together, half on each side. The two colours of paint will sit side by side without mixing.

3 Paint the wall, applying the roller at a variety of different angles to blend the two colours.

4 When complete, roller over the wall a few times to blend the paint further, but don't overwork.

OTHER COLOURS

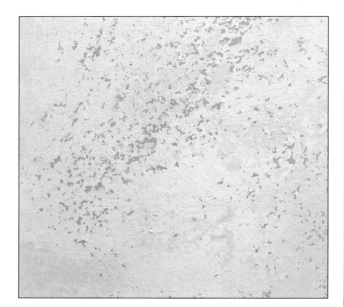

ABOVE: Alternative colours – yellow and cream emulsion (latex) over a dark turquoise base coat.

ABOVE: Complementary colours – light and mid-blue emulsion (latex) over a pale green base coat.

STONE WALL

A subtle stone effect is created using several different techniques. Layers of paint are built up by stippling, sponging and rubbing colours on and off, and a hog softening brush is used to blend the wet glazes to look like stone. The wall is divided by a trompe l'oeil dado (chair) rail.

You will need

- large decorator's paintbrush
- emulsion (latex) paint in cream
- spirit level
- ruler
- pencil
- masking tape
- acrylic paint in raw umber, white and yellow ochre
- acrylic scumble
- decorator's block brush or stippling brush
- natural sponge
- hog softening brush
- clean cotton cloths
- fine artist's paintbrush

1 Using a large decorator's paintbrush, paint the wall with cream emulsion (latex). Leave to dry.

2 Using a level and ruler, draw pencil lines 6.5cm/2½in apart at dado (chair) rail height.

3 Place masking tape inside the two pencil lines, smoothing it in place with your fingers.

4 Mix a glaze of 1 part raw umber acrylic paint to 6 parts scumble. Stipple this on to the wall, using the tip of the decorator's block brush or stippling brush. Do not stipple over the masked area. Leave to dry.

5 Mix a glaze with the white acrylic paint in the same way. Dampen a sponge and apply the glaze over the stippling, varying your hand position to avoid a uniform effect.

6 Using a hog softening brush, skim gently over the surface of the white glaze while it is still wet.

7 Mix a glaze with the yellow ochre paint as in step 4, but this time rub it into the wall with a cloth. Leave some areas of white glaze showing.

8 Using another dampened cloth, rub some areas to disperse the paint. Leave to dry.

9 Using a pencil and ruler, draw in the main lines of the false dado rail. Follow the illustration or copy a piece of moulding.

10 Highlight the pencil lines in white acrylic paint, using a fine artist's paintbrush. Leave to dry.

11 Paint the darker areas of the trompe l'oeil dado rail in raw umber acrylic paint. Leave to dry. Mix a little white acrylic paint into the raw umber and then add the softer, shadowed areas.

WAX-RESIST SHUTTERS

Give new wooden shutters or doors a weatherworn look by applying wax between two layers of different-coloured paint. Two colourways are shown – creamy yellow beneath bright blue, and pastel blue over candy pink for a sunny Caribbean feel.

You will need

- acrylic primer in white
- medium and small decorator's paintbrushes
- matt emulsion (flat latex) paint in soft yellow and bright blue or candy pink and pale blue
- neutral wax
- medium-grade abrasive paper

1 Paint the shutters with a coat of white primer and leave to dry. Then paint with soft yellow emulsion (latex). Leave to dry.

2 Using a small decorator's paintbrush, apply wax in areas that would naturally receive wear and tear such as the edges of the boards. Leave to dry.

3 Paint all over the shutters with bright blue emulsion, covering the waxed areas. Leave to dry.

4 Sand over the waxed areas to reveal the yellow base colour and create the "worn" effect.

ALTERNATIVE COLOURWAY

ABOVE: *For an alternative colourway, apply candy pink matt emulsion (flat latex) paint over the primer.*

ABOVE: *Apply wax as described in step 2, then paint with a pale blue top coat. Rub back with abrasive paper to reveal pink areas.*

KITCHEN TILES

These clever "tiles" are, in fact, simple squares painted using three different techniques. Fine tape separates the tiles and is removed at the end to give the illusion of grouting. You can experiment with other paint effects (see Painting Techniques) and colours to create your own design, or leave some of the squares white as a contrast.

You will need

- satin-finish emulsion (latex) paint in white
- standard-size paint roller and tray
- ruler and pencil
- spirit level
- masking tape
- fine line tape or car striping tape
- wide easy-mask decorator's tape
- emulsion (latex) paint in ultramarine blue
- small paint roller and tray
- natural sponge
- kitchen paper
- 4cm/1½in wide decorator's paintbrush
- mutton cloth (stockinet)
- craft knife (optional)

1 Paint the wall white, using a paint roller for an even texture. Decide on the width of your tiled panel. Mark the wall 45cm/18in above your work surface and in the centre of the width measurement.

2 Draw a horizontal pencil line across the width of the panel at this height, using a spirit level to make sure that it is straight. Place a strip of masking tape to sit above this line.

3 Mark dots along the tape at 15cm/6in intervals either side of the centre mark. Use the spirit level to draw vertical lines down the wall. Mark vertical dots at 15cm/6in intervals and draw horizontal lines.

4 Place fine line or car striping tape over the lines in both directions. Smooth the tape into place with your fingers, pressing it down well to ensure that as little paint as possible will be able to seep underneath it.

5 Place easy-mask tape around one square. Pour blue paint into a small paint tray and add 25 per cent water. Apply an even coat of paint to the roller, then roll it over the square. Repeat for all the plain blue squares.

6 Mask off a square to be sponged. Dampen the sponge in water, dip it into the blue paint and dab the excess on to some kitchen paper. Sponge the paint on the square. Repeat the same process for all the sponged squares.

7 Mask off a square to be dabbed with the mutton cloth (stockinet). Using a brush, apply the paint and then use the cloth to blend it. Continue other dabbed squares as before.

8 Remove all the tape and clean off the pencil marks. If any paint has seeped under the tape in places, use a craft knife to scrape it off, leaving a clean finish.

FROTTAGE HALLWAY

The technique of texturing paint by pressing tissue paper over the wet surface is known as "frottage". Here, tone-on-tone in soft green creates a delicate effect at the top of the hallway. The pattern in the textured wallpaper below the dado (chair) rail has been highlighted by stippling on a darker green glaze, then wiping it off with a cloth.

You will need

- satin-finish emulsion (latex) paint in light, medium and dark shades of soft green and white (buy a dark shade of the green paint and mix it with white to make the medium and light shades)
- large and medium decorator's paintbrushes
- matt emulsion (flat latex) paint in medium shade of soft green
- tissue paper
- acrylic scumble
- stippling brush
- clean cotton cloth

1 Paint the upper part of the wall with two coats of light green satin-finish paint, leaving each to dry.

2 Dilute the matt (flat) green paint with about 20 per cent water. Brush this on to a section of the wall.

3 Immediately press a sheet of tissue paper over the entire surface except for a narrow band adjacent to the next section you will be working. Work on a manageable area at a time so that you can keep the edge wet. Better still, ask someone to assist you – one brushing, one following with the tissue paper.

4 Carefully peel back the tissue paper to reveal most of the base colour underneath. Repeat over the rest of the upper part of the wall, using a fresh sheet of tissue paper on each section of your work.

5 Brush on two coats of medium green silk finish paint over the textured wallpaper below the dado (chair) rail, leaving each to dry. If the wallpaper is new, it may bubble, but it will shrink back when dry.

6 Mix the dark green silk finish paint with acrylic scumble in a ratio of 1 part paint to 6 parts scumble. Brush this glaze on to a section of the wallpaper.

7 Immediately dab over the wet glaze with a stippling brush to eliminate the brushmarks and even out the texture.

8 Wipe a cotton cloth gently over the stippled glaze to remove the glaze from the raised areas of the wallpaper. Complete the lower part of the wall section by section. Leave to dry. Paint the dado rail with white paint, leave to dry and then brush over the dark green glaze.

VINEGAR-GLAZED FLOORCLOTH

Painted floorcloths were fashionable with the early American settlers, and they remain popular as inexpensive, handmade alternatives to carpets. This one is painted with vinegar glaze and decorated with patterns, using a cork and other simple objects as stamps. Dark shellac gives the finished floorcloth an antique finish.

You will need

- heavyweight cotton duck canvas (from artist's suppliers), 7.5cm/3in larger all round than the finished floorcloth
- staple gun or hammer and tacks
- acrylic wood primer in white
- large and medium decorator's paintbrushes
- fine-grade abrasive paper
- set square (T square)
- pencil
- large scissors
- PVA (white) glue and brush
- 2.5cm/1in masking tape
- dessertspoon
- emulsion (latex) paint in bright red
- gloss acrylic floor varnish and brush – use matt (flat) acrylic varnish if preferred
- 1cm/½in masking tape
- malt vinegar
- sugar
- bowl and spoon
- powder pigment in dark ultramarine
- reusable putty adhesive
- clean cotton cloth
- craft knife
- cork
- dark shellac and brush
- floor varnish and brush

PREPARATION

Before beginning this project, stretch the canvas across an old door or table top and staple or tack it in place. Paint the surface with three or four coats of primer, leaving to dry between coats, then sand to give a completely smooth surface. Using a set square (T square), check that the canvas is square – if not, trim it down. Mark a pencil border 2.5cm/1in from the edge. Cut diagonally across each corner, through the point where the pencil lines cross.

1 Fold over each edge to the pencil line. Glue and then secure with masking tape until dry. Rub the edges firmly with a dessertspoon. Sand the edges where the primer has cracked.

2 Turn the canvas to the right side. Using masking tape, mark a wide border. Paint with bright red emulsion (latex), carrying the paint over the outer edges. When dry, apply a coat of floor varnish. Leave to dry.

3 Remove the masking tape and tidy any ragged edges with extra paint. When dry, place 1cm/½in masking tape around the outer edge to a depth of 1cm/½in. Repeat around the inner edge of the border.

4 Mix 150 ml/¼ pint/⅝ cup malt vinegar with 1 teaspoon sugar. Add up to 2 tablespoons of dark ultramarine powder pigment and stir well – the glaze should be of a consistency to flow on smoothly. Paint the glaze over the top of the red border.

5 While the dark ultramarine glaze is still wet, make patterns by pressing the reusable putty adhesive on top and then removing it.

6 Copy the patterns shown in the illustrations or experiment with your own. Wipe the glaze with a damp cotton cloth if you make a mistake. The glaze will take about 15 minutes to dry.

7 Using a craft knife, cut a hole in one end of the cork. Paint the dark ultramarine vinegar glaze over the centre panel. While the glaze is still wet, stamp a pattern of circles and lines.

8 Cut a square at the other end of the cork to make a different stamp. Experiment with other objects. Use the reusable putty adhesive to make additional lines and curves.

9 When the glaze is dry, remove the masking tape. Tidy the edges with a damp cloth wound around your finger. Apply a coat of dark shellac, then several coats of floor varnish, allowing the canvas to dry between coats. Leave the floorcloth for at least 4 days before walking on it.

COMBED CHECK FLOOR

A simple combing technique has been used to decorate this warm, sunny floor. You can experiment with other patterns instead of the traditional wave pattern shown here. Using a hardboard template to draw the squares saves the chore of measuring and marking out the floor before you start.

You will need

- emulsion (latex) paint in yellow ochre, orange and red
- medium decorator's paintbrush
- 30cm/12in wide piece of hardboard
- pencil
- masking tape
- acrylic scumble
- rubber comb
- acrylic floor varnish and brush

1 Paint the floor with two coats of yellow ochre emulsion (latex), leaving each to dry thoroughly.

2 Starting in the corner most on view, place the piece of hardboard against the side of the wall. Draw pencil lines widthways across the room. Return to the same corner and draw lines lengthways to form a grid.

3 Place masking tape on the outside of alternate lines, both horizontally and vertically, to prepare for the first colour of squares.

4 Mix some scumble into the orange emulsion. Paint this mixture on to one square (you will need to work on one at a time so that the paint remains wet).

5 Run the rubber comb through the wet paint, twisting your hand slightly to form a wave pattern. Repeat the process with the orange squares on alternate rows. Leave to dry, then remove the masking tape.

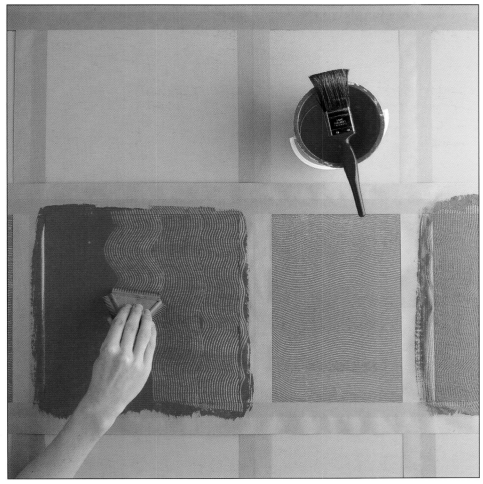

6 Place masking tape the other side of those squares previously marked. Paint these, one at a time, with red emulsion mixed with scumble.

7 Run the comb through the wet paint, this time in the opposite direction. Half the squares on the floor will now be painted.

8 To complete the remaining squares, simply mask each square individually and then paint in the appropriate colour.

9 Comb each of the squares as you go, while the paint is still wet. While combing, vary the direction of the wave pattern as before.

10 When the paint is dry, seal the floor with three coats of acrylic floor varnish. Leave to dry thoroughly before walking on the floor.

DISTRESSED TABLE TOP

A second-hand buy can be transformed with a fashionably distressed look in shades of blue paint. Petroleum jelly and candle wax resist the paint in different ways. The petroleum jelly is applied to the table top in the main areas of natural wear and tear; the candle wax is then used, giving a more subtle effect.

You will need

- sanding block and medium-grade abrasive paper
- emulsion (latex) paint in navy blue, pale blue and mid-blue
- small decorator's paintbrush
- petroleum jelly and brush
- clean cotton cloth
- candle
- matt (flat) acrylic varnish and brush

1 Sand the table top to provide a key for the paint.

2 Paint with the navy blue emulsion (latex). Leave to dry.

3 Brush blobs of petroleum jelly on to the table top, working inwards from the edges of the table.

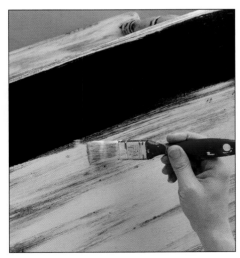

4 Paint the table top with pale blue emulsion, applying the brushstrokes in the same direction – don't cover the surface completely. Leave to dry.

5 Wipe over with a cloth and soapy water. In the areas where the petroleum jelly has been applied, the pale blue paint will come away, revealing the navy blue base coat.

6 Rub over the surface of the table with candle wax, concentrating on the edges of the table top and areas where there would be natural wear and tear.

7 Paint the table with mid-blue emulsion, again applying the brushstrokes in the same direction. Leave to dry.

8 Rub over the surface with abrasive paper. Where the candle wax has been applied, the mid-blue paint will be removed. Seal the table with two coats of varnish.

DRY-BRUSHED CHAIR

A soft, distressed look is achieved by dry brushing off-white paint over a light brown base painted to imitate wood. This is another excellent technique for making a tired old piece of furniture look desirably aged.

You will need

- clean cotton cloth
- sanding block and medium-grade abrasive paper
- emulsion (latex) paint in pale terracotta and off-white
- small decorator's paintbrush
- sponge
- matt (flat) acrylic varnish and brush

1 Wipe over the chair with a damp cloth, then sand it in the direction of the grain.

2 Mix the pale terracotta emulsion (latex) 50/50 with water. Paint the whole chair.

3 While the paint is still wet, use a sponge dampened with water to remove the excess paint mixture carefully.

4 Using a dry brush, apply the off-white emulsion over the chair. At the angles, flick the paint from the base upwards.

5 For the flat surfaces, hold the brush at an angle and apply the paint with minimal pressure. Leave to dry then seal with two coats of varnish, leaving to dry between coats.

GRAINED DOOR

This strongly textured combed graining is achieved by mixing wall filler with sky blue emulsion (latex). Lime green paint is then brushed over the blue and sanded off when dry to give a surprisingly subtle effect.

You will need

- medium-grade abrasive paper
- emulsion (latex) paint in sky blue and lime green
- medium decorator's paintbrush
- wall filler
- rubber comb
- matt (flat) acrylic varnish and brush

1 Using medium-grade abrasive paper, sand the door to provide a key for the paint. Paint the surface with a base coat of sky blue emulsion (latex). Leave to dry.

2 Mix 25 per cent filler with 75 per cent sky blue paint. Paint on, working on a small section at a time. While still wet, comb lines, following the grain. Leave to dry.

3 Paint the door with a thin coat of lime green emulsion, applying the paint in the same direction as the combing to follow the grain of the wood. Leave to dry.

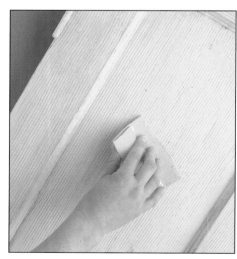

4 Sand the door, revealing lines of sky blue paint beneath the lime green top coat. Seal with two coats of acrylic varnish.

HARLEQUIN SCREEN

Two simple paint techniques – stippling and rag rolling – are used here to great effect. Choose bright shades of paint as the colours will be softened by the white-tinted scumble glaze.

You will need

- three-panel screen with curved top
- screwdriver
- emulsion (latex) paint in cream
- medium decorator's brush
- fine-grade abrasive paper
- 1cm/½in wide masking tape
- 1cm/½in wide flexible masking tape
- long ruler or straight piece of wood
- water-soluble marker pencil
- fine line tape or car striping tape
- wide easy-mask decorator's tape
- stencil brush
- kitchen paper
- white palette or old white plate
- emulsion (latex) paint in turquoise, red, yellow and green
- matt (flat) varnish and brush
- acrylic paint in white
- acrylic scumble
- clean cotton cloth
- acrylic paint in gold
- gouache paint in gold
- small stencil brush

PREPARATION

It is best to remove the hinges before sanding the surfaces to be decorated. Apply cream emulsion (latex) and leave to dry, then sand to give a smooth surface. Refer to the artwork at the back of the book for templates of how to mark up the screen.

1 Place masking tape close to the edge of the screen along the outer borders of the two outer panels, and along the base of all three panels. Place a second line of tape next to the first.

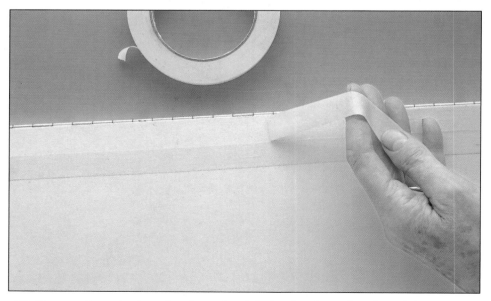

2 Remove the outer tape, leaving a 1cm/½in border along the edge of the screen. Smooth down the remaining tape. Using flexible masking tape, repeat steps 1 and 2 along the top of all three panels.

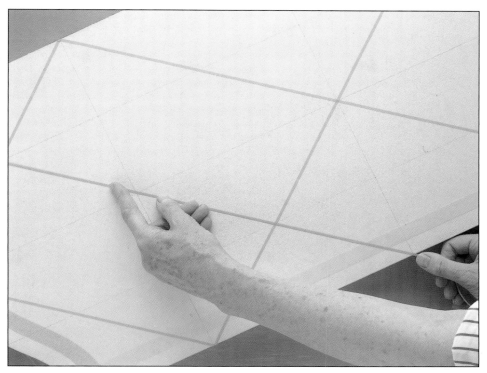

3 Measure the height of the screen at the longest point and divide by six. Draw a vertical line halfway across the panel. Mark the centre point and two equally spaced points either side. Return to the centre point and divide the panel horizontally into four equal points, one each side of the central line. Draw a grid of equal-sized oblongs, four across and six down. Repeat for the other panels.

4 Lay fine line tape or car striping tape from the centre point at the top of each panel diagonally to the far right-hand corner of the next space. Continue from the far right-hand corner through the centre point until all the lines are marked with tape. Repeat in the opposite direction to make a diamond pattern. Secure the tape at the sides of the panel with a small piece of masking tape.

5 Using wide easy-mask decorator's tape, mask off the diamonds that are to be painted in the first colour. Follow the picture of the finished screen for colour reference.

6 Bind 2.5cm/1in at the base of the stencil brush with masking tape. Dip the brush into the first colour, wipe the surplus on kitchen paper until the brush is fairly dry, then stipple the masked diamonds. Work out to the masking tape, using a firm pouncing motion. Leave to dry. Using the other colours, stipple all the diamonds in the same way.

8 Holding a crumpled cloth between both hands, roll it down each panel while the glaze is still wet, moving your hands in different directions. Leave the glaze to dry.

7 When all the paint is dry, remove the fine line or car striping tape. Apply a coat of matt (flat) varnish and leave to dry. Mix a little white acrylic paint into the scumble to make a glaze. Paint this over the diamonds.

10 Mix both gold paints together. Lay masking tape either side of the cream borders. Stipple the gold paint on with a small stencil brush. Leave to dry, then remove the masking tape. Apply a final coat of varnish. When dry, replace the screen hinges.

9 Apply another coat of varnish. When this is dry, remove the masking tape from the borders of the diamonds.

GRAINED WINDOW FRAME

Here, extra interest is added to a window frame by decorating it with a subtle imitation wood pattern. The same treatment would work well on a wide picture frame. To hide a boring view, stencil the panes of glass with frosted stars.

You will need

- medium-grade abrasive paper
- vinyl silk paint in pale blue-green
- medium decorator's paintbrush
- matt emulsion (flat latex) paint in deep blue-green
- water-based scumble
- heart grainer (rocker)
- clean cotton cloth
- gloss acrylic varnish and brush
- rubber comb
- star stencil
- masking tape
- stencil brush
- acrylic frosting varnish

1 Sand the window frame with medium-grade abrasive paper, then paint with pale blue-green vinyl silk paint and leave to dry. For the glaze, mix 1 part deep blue-green emulsion (latex) to 6 parts scumble. Paint the glaze over the main surfaces.

2 While the glaze is wet, draw the heart grainer (rocker) across the glazed surface, rocking it backwards and forwards. Wipe the corners with a damp cloth to make a mitre. As you work, protect the wet graining with a piece of abrasive paper. Leave to dry.

3 Apply a coat of varnish only over the glazed areas and leave to dry. Paint the inner edges of the frame and the glazing bars across the window with glaze. While still wet, draw down each piece of wood with a rubber comb. Leave to dry, then apply another coat of varnish over the whole window frame.

4 Make sure that the glass is clean, then attach the stencil with masking tape. Using a stencil brush, apply the frosting varnish evenly through the stencil. Remove the stencil before the varnish dries completely.

CRACKLE-GLAZE PICTURE FRAME

This simple picture frame – which could also be used to hold a small mirror – is made from a piece of plywood. Simply cut a square from the centre and edge with beading. As well as being treated with crackle glaze, the brightly coloured paintwork is distressed slightly with abrasive paper to give a very attractive finish.

You will need

- emulsion (latex) paint in yellow ochre, turquoise, orange, lime green and bright pink
- medium and small decorator's brushes
- acrylic crackle glaze
- masking tape
- craft knife
- flat artist's paintbrush
- coarse-grade abrasive paper
- acrylic varnish and brush

1 Paint the frame with two coats of yellow ochre emulsion (latex), allowing each to dry. Brush on a coat of crackle glaze. Leave to dry according to the manufacturer's instructions.

2 Place strips of masking tape in a pattern on either side of the frame, as shown.

3 Where the ends of the masking tape overlap, carefully trim off the excess tape with a craft knife.

5 Brush orange paint on alternate sections of the pattern in the same way. Paint the remaining sections lime green. Leave to dry.

4 Brush turquoise paint on the unmasked sections of the frame, working in one direction. The crackle effect will appear almost immediately. Take care not to overbrush an area (see Painting Techniques).

6 Carefully peel away the masking tape, revealing the yellow ochre base coat.

7 Using a flat artist's paintbrush, apply bright pink paint to the areas where the masking tape had been. Do this freehand to give the frame a handpainted look. Leave to dry.

8 Rub coarse-grade abrasive paper over the whole of the picture frame to show some of the yellow ochre paint beneath the brightly coloured surface.

9 Seal the frame with two coats of acrylic varnish. Apply the first coat quickly, taking care not to overbrush and reactivate the crackle glaze.

SPONGED LAMP BASE

Three shades of green paint are sponged on to this inexpensive lamp base to give a very attractive dappled surface. If you prefer, you can practise the sponging technique first on a piece of white paper until you are confident. You will quickly discover that it is not at all difficult, despite the very professional-looking result.

You will need

- wooden lamp base with electric cord and bulb fitting
- masking tape
- scissors
- rubber gloves
- fine wire (steel) wool
- acrylic primer
- flat artist's paintbrush
- emulsion (latex) paint in off-white, jade green and emerald green
- bowl
- natural sponge
- white paper
- clear acrylic varnish and brush

1 Cover the electric cord and bulb fitting with layers of masking tape to protect them while you work.

2 Wearing rubber gloves, rub down the existing varnish or paint with wire (steel) wool.

3 Using a flat artist's paintbrush, paint the lamp base with two coats of acrylic primer, leaving each to dry.

4 Paint with two coats of off-white emulsion (latex), leaving the paint to dry between coats.

5 Mix a 50/50 solution of jade green emulsion paint and water. Dampen the sponge and squeeze it until nearly dry, then dip it into the paint. Practise by dabbing the sponge on to a piece of white paper.

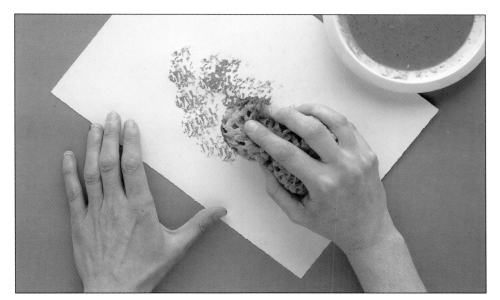

6 Cover the lamp base with a dappled layer of paint, applying it just a little at a time in order to build up the texture gradually.

7 Add some off-white paint to lighten the jade green colour. Sponge this lightly over the first layer of colour. Break off a small piece of sponge and use this to work the colour into the moulding to ensure that the whole lamp base is evenly covered.

8 Mix a little emerald green paint 50/50 with water. Apply this mixture sparingly over the surface of the lamp base to add extra depth and texture. When dry, seal with three coats of varnish, allowing the varnish to dry thoroughly between coats. Finally, remove the protective masking tape from the electric cord and bulb fitting.

CRACKLE-GLAZE PLANTER

Here, crackle glaze is sandwiched between dark and pale layers of emulsion (latex) paint to give a modern planter an authentic antique look. The handpainted line is easier to do than you might think, and gives a smart finishing touch.

You will need

- MDF (medium-density fiberboard) planter
- fine-grade abrasive paper (optional)
- emulsion (latex) paint in mid-blue and dark cream
- small decorator's paintbrush
- acrylic crackle glaze
- fine artist's paintbrush
- clear acrylic varnish and brush

1 You do not need to prime MDF (medium-density fiberboard), but it may need sanding. Paint the inside and outside with mid-blue emulsion (latex).

2 When the paint is completely dry, apply a layer of crackle glaze to the outside of the planter. Leave to dry.

3 Paint the outside of the planter with dark cream emulsion. The crackled effect will start to appear almost immediately, so work quickly, with regular brushstrokes. Leave to dry.

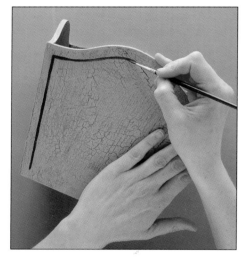

4 Holding your finger against the edge for support, paint a thin mid-blue line 1.5cm/⅝in from the edge on each side of the planter. Leave to dry, then seal with two coats of varnish.

SCANDINAVIAN TABLE

This pretty little table has been distressed by rubbing back thin layers of colour with fine wire (steel) wool. Focusing on the areas that would normally suffer most from general wear and tear gives an authentic aged look. The simple leaf design is painted freehand and picked out with paler highlights.

You will need

- MDF (medium-density fiberboard) or wooden table with drawer
- rubber gloves
- fine wire (steel) wool
- emulsion (latex) paint in dark yellow, grey-green, white, mid-green and pale green
- flat artist's paintbrush
- small decorator's paintbrushes
- acrylic scumble
- fine artist's paintbrush
- clear matt (flat) acrylic varnish and brush

1 Rub down the table with fine wire (steel) wool, wearing a pair of rubber gloves. Pay particular attention to the bevelled edges.

2 Using dark yellow emulsion (latex) and a flat artist's paintbrush, paint the mouldings (if any) around the edge of the drawer and the table top.

3 Paint the rest of the table and the drawer front with two coats of grey-green emulsion, allowing the paint to dry between coats.

4 Wearing rubber gloves once again, rub down the entire surface of the table with wire wool. Concentrate on the areas that would naturally suffer from wear and tear.

5 Mix 50/50 white emulsion and scumble. Apply sparsely to the grey-green areas with a dry brush, using light diagonal strokes and varying the angle of the brush to give an even coverage over the surface.

6 Mix 50/50 dark yellow emulsion and scumble. Paint this over the mouldings.

7 Apply light dabs of mid-green paint to the parts of the table that would receive the most wear: the top corners of the legs and underneath. Leave to dry, then rub back with wire wool.

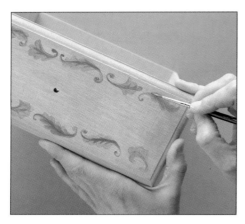

8 Using a fine artist's paintbrush, paint a scrolling leaf design around the edge of the drawer front in pale green. Pick out the stalks and leaf veins with fine brushstrokes in mid-green.

9 Still using the fine artist's paintbrush, add white and dark yellow highlights to the leaf design. Leave to dry.

10 Seal the drawer and table with a coat of clear matt (flat) acrylic varnish for protection.

STENCILLING

Stencilling is often the first paint effect that people try and it is one of the most enduring and popular of home decorating techniques. Whether you use it boldly in place of wallpaper or simply to add decorative details to walls, furniture and other household objects, you can be sure of achieving an eye-catching effect. You will be surprised at how quickly you can transform even a very large surface with a striking pattern. The joy of stencils is that they can be applied to almost any surface, from fabrics and floors to glass and walls. Although you can buy stencils from do-it-yourself stores and other specialist shops, it is much more rewarding and fun to make your own.

ABOVE: A simple sandcastle stencil is given extra vitality with handpainted flagpoles.

LEFT: A richly ornate wall design is echoed on a matching cushion stencilled with gold fabric paint.

STENCILLING MATERIALS

Avariety of materials can be used for stencilling, from specialist stencilling paints and sticks to acrylics and emulsion (latex). Each has its own properties and will create different effects.

Acrylic stencil paints

These are quick-drying paints, reducing the chance of the paint running and seeping behind the stencil. Acrylic stencil paints are available in a wide range of colours and can be mixed to create more subtle shades.

Acrylic varnish

This is useful for sealing and protecting finished projects.

Emulsion paints

Ordinary household emulsion (latex) can also be used for stencilling. It is best to avoid the cheaper varieties as these contain a lot of water and will seep through the stencil.

Fabric paints

These are used in the same way as acrylic stencil paints, and come in an equally wide range of colours, which can be mixed to create your own shades. Fixed with an iron according to the manufacturer's instructions, they will withstand washing and everyday use. As with ordinary acrylic stencil paints do not overload the brush with colour, as it will seep into the fabric. Always back the fabric you are stencilling with scrap paper or newspaper to prevent the paints from marking the work surface.

Gold leaf and gold size

These can be used to spectacular effect. The actual design is stencilled with gold size. The size is then left to become tacky and the gold leaf rubbed over the design.

Metallic creams

These are available in many different metallic finishes, from gold through to bronze and copper and silver. Metallic creams can be applied as highlights on a painted base, or used for the entire design. They can be applied with cloths or your fingertip.

Oil-based stencil sticks and creams

The sticks can be used in the same way as a wax crayon, while the creams can be applied with a brush, cloth or your fingertip. With any method, there is no danger of overloading the colour, and they won't run. The disadvantage is their long drying time (can be overnight in some cases); also, the colours can become muddy when mixed. Sticks and creams are also available for use on fabrics.

RIGHT: 1 acrylic stencil paints, 2 oil-based cream and metallic creams, 3 fabric paints, 4 oil-based stencil sticks, 5 emulsion (latex) paints, 6 gold leaf, 7 acrylic varnish, 8 gold size.

STENCILLING EQUIPMENT

Stencilling does not require a great deal of specialist equipment; many of the items used are commonly found in most households. Some additional items, however, will make the job easier.

Brushes

It is worth investing in a set of good stencil brushes. The ends of the brushes should be flat and the bristles firm, to allow you to control the application of paint. A medium-sized brush (3cm/1$\frac{1}{2}$in diameter) is a useful, all-purpose size, but you may want to buy one size smaller and one size larger as well. You will need a selection of household paintbrushes for applying large areas of background colour, and small artist's paintbrushes for adding fine details.

Craft knife

Use for cutting out stencils from card (stock).

Self-healing cutting mat

This provides a firm surface to cut into and will help prevent the craft knife from slipping. Mats come in a range of sizes and are commonly printed with a grid and imperial or metric measures for accurate and quick cutting.

Masking tape

As the stencil may need to be repositioned it is advisable to hold it in place with masking tape, which can be removed fairly easily.

Paint-mixing container

This may be necessary for mixing paints and colourwashes.

Pencils

Keep a selection of both soft and hard pencils to transfer the stencil design on to card (stock). Use an ordinary pencil to mark the positions of the stencils before applying.

Stencil card

The material used to make the stencil is a matter of personal preference. Special stencil card (stock) is available waxed, which means that it will last longer, but ordinary card or heavy paper can also be used. It is worth purchasing a sheet of clear acetate if you wish to keep your stencil design. This means that you will be able to reuse the design for future projects.

Tape measure and straight-edges

Many stencilling projects require accurate positioning. Measuring and planning the design and layout of your stencils before you begin will aid the result.

Tracing paper

Use this to transfer your stencil design on to stencil card (stock).

RIGHT: 1 sraight-edges, 2 tape measure, 3 stencil brushes, 4 household paintbrush, 5 self-healing cutting mat, 6 stencil card (stock), 7 tracing paper, 8 soft pencil, 9 craft knife, 10 paint-mixing container, 11 masking tape.

STENCILLING TECHNIQUES

Stencilling is not difficult to master, but it is worth practising on a small area to get used to handling the stencil brush and to become accustomed to the properties of the various paints you use. The techniques illustrated below show you how to make your own stencils and different ways in which to use them.

TRANSFERRING TEMPLATES

1 To transfer a template on to a piece of stencil card (stock), place a piece of tracing paper over the design, and draw over it with a hard pencil.

2 Turn over the tracing paper, and on the back of the design rub over the lines you have drawn, this time using a soft pencil.

3 Turn the design back to the right side and place on a sheet of stencil card. Draw over the original lines with a hard pencil.

CUTTING STENCILS

1 Place the tracing paper design on to a self-healing cutting mat or piece of thick card (stock) and secure in place with masking tape. Use a craft knife for cutting along the pencil lines.

2 It is safer to move the cutting board towards you and the craft knife when you are working round awkward shapes. Continue to cut out the design, moving the board as necessary.

STENCILLING EFFECTS

Block stencilling in a single solid colour

Use for filling in large areas in a single solid colour. As in all stencilling, remember not to apply the paint too heavily – less is more. Always blot out the paint on to a piece of blotting card (stock) before you begin.

Block stencilling with second colour stippled

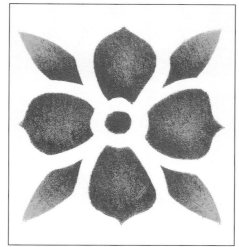

When applying two colours, always apply the lighter shade first, then the darker. Do not cover the entire surface with the first colour; leave a gap for the second shade, then blend later. Use a separate, clean brush for each colour.

Block stencilling in two colours

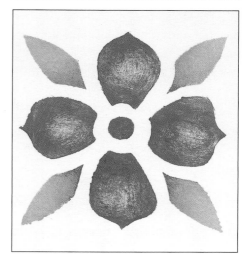

When you apply the first colour, do not fully block out the petals; instead, outline them with the first colour and leave the centres bare. Use the second colour to fill. Take care not to apply the paint too heavily.

Rotating with blocked leaves

Using a very dry brush with a tiny amount of paint, rotate the bristles in a circular motion. This rotating action leaves enough paint on the surface for a lighter, softer look than a block application. Use the same effect in a darker colour on the inside of the petals.

Rotating and soft shading

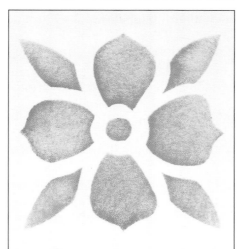

Using a very dry brush with a tiny amount of paint, place your brush on one side of the stencil and rotate the brush in small circles. Repeat this action, using a slightly darker colour on the edges of the stencil, to create the effect of soft shading.

Rotating and shading in two colours

This is a similar effect to rotating and shading, but is more directional. Using a very dry brush with a tiny amount of paint, place your brush in the centre of the flower and rotate the bristles slightly outwards. Repeat this action, using a slightly darker colour.

Brushing up and down

Using slightly more paint on your brush than you would for rotating, brush up and down only, taking care to keep the lines vertical.

Dry brushing with curve

Using the rotating technique, start at the centre of the design and work outwards in big circles.

Dry brushing and rotating

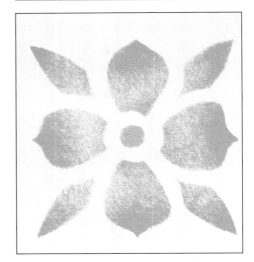

Apply a tiny amount of paint by rotating the bristles from the centre, and from the outside tips, to give more paint in these areas. Work along the line, using less pressure than on the centre and the tips. This gives a softer effect on the areas in between.

Rotating brush with leaves flicked

Fill in the petals by rotating a very dry brush and a tiny amount of paint. For the flicking effect on the leaves, use slightly more paint on the brush. Working from the centre, flick the paint outwards once or twice. Do not overdo.

Dry brushing, rotating from edge

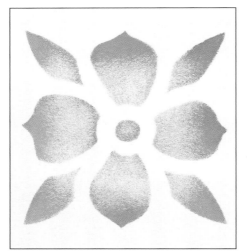

Using big circular strokes, work from the outside of the whole stencil, moving inwards. This should leave you with more paint on the outside, as there will be less and less paint on your brush as you move inwards.

Brushing up and down from the sides

This is similar to flicking. Using slightly more paint on your brush than you would for rotating, brush up and down, then from side to side. Keep the brushmarks vertical and horizontal to give a lined effect.

Rough stippling

This method uses more paint and less pressure than rotating or flicking. Taking a reasonable amount of paint on the bristles of your brush, simply place it down lightly. This gives a rougher look. Do not go over it too many times as this spoils the effect.

Two-colour stippling

Use less paint than for rough stippling. The second colour is stippled out from the centre, to blend with the first colour.

One-sided stippling

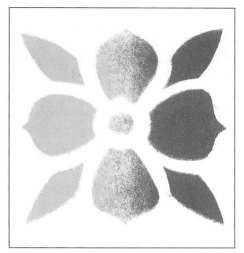

Apply the lighter colour first, up to a point just past the centre. Apply the darker colour, and stipple to the centre. Always start on the outer edge so that you leave more paint on the edges of the stencil design.

Stippling with a dry brush

This is similar to stippling, except that it is essential to dab most of the paint off the bristles before you start. This gives a softer stippling effect.

Gentle stippling from the edges

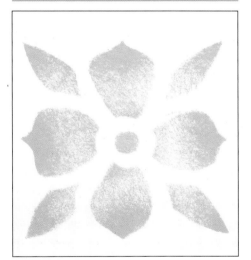

Using a very dry brush (dab most of the paint off the bristles before you start), stipple from the outside, working inwards. By the time you get to the centre, there should be hardly any paint left on your brush, ensuring a very soft paint effect in this area.

Stippling to shade with two colours

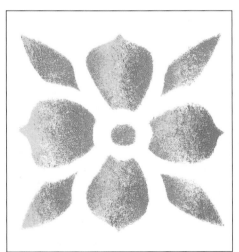

Using a reasonable amount of paint, apply the lighter shade first. Apply the darker shade to one side only of each window. (Here, the second colour is applied to the right-hand side.) A few dabs of the darker colour paint will be quite sufficient.

Flicking upwards with the brush

Using a reasonable amount of paint (not too wet or too dry) on your brush, flick upwards only. This creates a line at the top of the petals and leaves.

Flicking in two directions, up and down

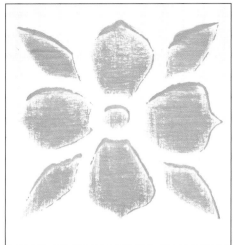

Using a reasonable amount of paint on your brush, flick up and down. Do not use too much paint as it will collect on the edges of the petals and leaves.

Flicking from the outside to the centre

Using a reasonable amount of paint on your brush, flick from the outside edges in to the centre of the design. Flick from the top to the centre, from the bottom to the centre, from the left to the centre, and from the right to the centre.

Flicking from the top to the centre

Using a reasonable amount of paint on your brush, flick from the top edge of the window to the centre of the design, then from the bottom edge of the window to the centre.

Drop shadow, using a block effect

Apply the first colour, which should be the lighter shade, using a block effect. Concentrate on one side of each window (here, the right-hand side). Move the stencil slightly to the left – a few millimetres is sufficient – taking care not to move it up or down. Block again, using a darker colour, to create a drop shadow effect.

TIPS

Check the amount of paint on the stencil brush by practising on a piece of scrap paper. Excess paint can be removed by dabbing the brush on an old saucer or clean cotton cloth.

Clean the stencil brush before using a different colour to keep the colours fresh. It is a good idea to invest in several different-sized brushes.

If you want to use a different colour scheme to that shown in the project, for example to suit your existing decor, see Working with Colour at the beginning of the book for advice and inspiration.

Finally, do not aim for perfectly identical stencilled motifs. Much of the appeal of stencilling lies in its handpainted look and irregularities.

PENNSYLVANIA-DUTCH TULIPS

This American folk-art inspired idea uses the rich colours and simple motifs beloved by the German and Dutch immigrants to Pennsylvania. Create the effect of hand-painted wallpaper or, for a beginner's project, take a single motif and use it to decorate a small cabinet.

You will need

- emulsion (latex) paint in dark ochre
- large and small decorator's paintbrushes
- woodwash in indigo blue and mulberry
- stencil card (stock)
- craft knife and self-healing cutting mat
- pencil
- ruler
- stencil brushes
- stencil paint in red, light green, dark green and pale brown
- saucer or cloth
- artist's paintbrush

1 Dilute 1 part dark ochre emulsion (latex) with 1 part water. Using a large paintbrush, cover the top half of the wall with the diluted paint. Use vertical brushstrokes for an even texture.

2 Paint the lower half of the wall with indigo blue woodwash. Finish off with a curving line using a dry brush to suggest woodgrain.

3 Paint the dado (chair) rail or a strip at dado rail height in mulberry woodwash, using a narrow brush to give a clean edge.

4 Trace the tulip and heart templates at the back of the book and cut the stencils from stencil card (stock) as described in Stencilling Techniques. Mark the centre of each edge of the stencil. Measure the wall and divide it into equal sections, so that the repeats will fall at about 20cm/8in intervals. Mark the positions with pencil, so that they can be rubbed out later.

5 Dip a stencil brush into red stencil paint. Rub the brush on a saucer or cloth until it is almost dry before stencilling in the tulip flowers. Leave to dry.

6 Paint the leaves in light green stencil paint with dark green shading, using an artist's paintbrush. Paint the stems in dark green. Leave to dry.

7 Stencil the basket in pale brown stencil paint using a chunky stencil brush to give texture.

8 Stencil a single heart between each two baskets of tulips using red stencil paint. Judge the positioning of the hearts by eye to give a natural handpainted look.

ABOVE: Decorate a matching key cabinet following the same method and using a single motif.

ABOVE: A simple tulip motif stencilled kitchen storage tin gives instant folk-art style.

FRENCH COUNTRY KITCHEN

This curtain (drape) design is adapted from the pattern on a French Art Deco soup bowl found in a fleamarket in Brussels. The flower design is echoed in the hand-stencilled tiles and teams perfectly with the simple chequerboard border for a country look.

You will need

For the curtain (drape):
- white muslin (cheesecloth)
- iron
- newspaper
- masking tape
- stencil card (stock)
- craft knife and self-healing cutting mat
- spray adhesive
- solid stencil paint in blue
- stencil brush
- pressing cloth
- needle
- white sewing cotton
- tape measure
- dressmaker's chalk
- white cotton tape
- small pearl buttons

For the tiles:
- 10cm/4in square white tiles
- spray paint in red

MEASURING UP

To calculate the amount of muslin (cheesecloth), allow 1.5 times the width of the window plus 2.5cm/1in for each side hem, and add 7.5cm/3in to the length for hems.

1 Press the muslin (cheesecloth) to remove any creases, then fold it lengthways in accordion-style folds. Press lightly to mark creases, then fold it widthways in accordion-style folds and press again. These squares will act as a guide for positioning the motifs. Cover the work surface with newspaper and tape down the muslin so that it is taut.

2 Trace the three floral templates and the border template at the back of the book and cut out the stencils from stencil card (stock) as described in Stencilling Techniques. Spray the back of one stencil with adhesive and, starting at the top right, lightly stencil the first motif.

3 Alternating the three floral stencils as you work, lightly stencil flowers in every other square over the whole curtain (drape), leaving 15cm/6in free at the lower edge for the border.

4 Stencil the blue chequerboard border along the bottom, lining up the stencil each time by matching the last two squares of the previous motif with the first two of the next stencil. Press the fabric well using a pressing cloth and iron.

5 Press under and slip-stitch a 1.25cm/¹/₂in double hem around the sides and lower edge of the curtain. Make a 2.5cm/1in double hem along the top edge.

6 Measure the top edge of the curtain and, using dressmaker's chalk, mark it into sections about 20cm/8in apart. Cut a 25cm/10in piece of white cotton tape for each mark. Fold the first piece of tape in half and stitch to the back of the first mark. Sew a button on to the front of the curtain to anchor the tape. Repeat all the way along the edge and then tie the finished curtain on to the curtain pole in bows.

7 For the tiles, cut a piece of stencil card to fit the tile. Cut out the three floral stencils as before, using a craft knife and a self-healing cutting mat.

8 Wash the tiles in warm soapy water. Cover the work surface with newspaper. Using red spray paint, spray over the first floral stencil lightly and evenly. Leave to dry, then remove the stencil. Repeat with the other tiles, using all three stencils.

4 Lightly rub over the tray with abrasive paper to reveal some of the blue-grey paint underneath.

5 Trace the templates at the back of the book or draw around pressed leaves. Using a craft knife and self-healing cutting mat, cut out the stencils from stencil card (stock) as described in Stencilling Techniques.

ABOVE: Building up layers of paint and rubbing back the top layer in places gives the tray a pleasing distressed look.

6 Lightly spray the back of the stencils with adhesive. Arrange the stencils on the tray and smooth down. Dip the stencil brush into the rust stencil paint and rub it on a saucer or cloth so that the brush is dry. Using circular movements, apply the colour evenly over the stencils, working more on one side of each motif. Apply terracotta stencil paint to the other side of the leaves to give shadow. Continue stencilling all over the tray. To give the tray a tough finish, apply two or three coats of varnish, leaving each to dry before applying the next.

GILDED CANDLES

Plain church candles look extra special when adorned with simple gold stars and stripes. Always associated with Christmas, candles are popular all year round for their soft romantic lighting. Cutting the stencils may be fiddly but it is then a quick job to spray on the gold paint.

You will need

- acetate
- selection of candles
- felt-tipped pen
- craft knife and self-healing cutting mat
- spray adhesive
- masking tape
- metallic spray paint

1 Wrap a piece of acetate around the candle. Mark with a felt-tipped pen and cut it to fit exactly. Do not overlap the edges. Cut it a few millimetres shorter than the candle.

2 Trace the star templates at the back of the book. Lay the piece of acetate over the stars, choosing a pattern of stars to suit the candle. Trace over them with the felt-tipped pen.

3 Cut out the stars using a craft knife and self-healing cutting mat. Be careful not to tear the acetate.

4 Spray one side of the stencil with adhesive and wrap it around the candle, centring it so that there is a small gap at either end. Secure the acetate join with masking tape. Mask the top of the candle with tape, ensuring there are no gaps.

5 Spray a fine mist of metallic spray paint over the candle, holding the can about 30cm/12in from the surface. If too much paint is applied, it will drip underneath the stencil. Keep checking that the stencil is well stuck down to avoid any fuzzy lines around the stars. Leave the paint to dry for a couple of minutes, then carefully remove the masking tape and acetate.

6 For a stars and stripes candle, cut strips of acetate and trace a row of small stars along each strip. Cut out with a craft knife as before. Spray one side of the acetate strips with adhesive. Stick the strips on to the candle, measuring the gaps in between to ensure equal spacing. Secure them with small pieces of masking tape at the join.

7 Mask off the top of the candle with masking tape, ensuring there are no gaps. Spray the candle with a fine mist of metallic spray paint as in step 5. Carefully remove the masking tape and stencil when dry.

ABOVE: A basketful of gilded candles makes a pretty gift. Use a different star design on each candle.

8 For a reverse stencil design, cut out individual star shapes from acetate. Apply spray adhesive to one side, stick on to the candle and mask off the top of the candle as before. Spray with metallic spray paint and carefully remove the acetate stars when the paint is dry.

RENAISSANCE ART

Turn your hallway into a dramatic entrance with ornate stencils and rich colours. Combine them with gold accessories, antique furniture and velvets and braids to complete the theatrical setting. This design would also be ideal for creating an intimate dining room for candlelit dinners.

You will need

- ruler
- spirit level
- pencil
- masking tape
- emulsion (latex) paint in pale slate-blue, terracotta and pale peach
- sponges
- stencil brushes
- stencil card (stock)
- craft knife and self-healing cutting mat
- stencil paint in dark grey-blue, terracotta, emerald and turquoise

1 Using a ruler and spirit level, divide the wall in half horizontally with a pencil line, then draw a second line 15cm/6in above the first. Stick a line of masking tape just below this top line. Dilute 1 part slate-blue emulsion (latex) with 1 part water and colour the top half of the wall using a sponge.

2 Stick masking tape above the bottom pencil line. Dilute 1 part terracotta emulsion with 1 part water. Sponge over the lower half of the wall.

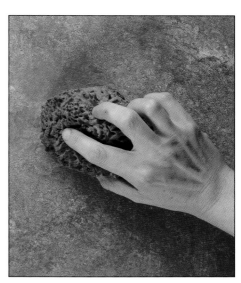

3 Sponge lightly over the terracotta sponging with pale slate-blue to add a textural effect. Remove the strips of masking tape.

4 Colour the centre band with diluted peach emulsion using a stencil brush. Trace the templates at the back of the book and cut out the stencils from stencil card (stock) using a craft knife and self-healing cutting mat.

5 Stencil the wall motifs at roughly regular intervals over the upper part of the wall, using dark grey-blue stencil paint. Rotate the stencil with every alternate motif to give movement to the design.

6 Starting at the right-hand side of the peach band, stencil the border motif with terracotta stencil paint. Add details in emerald and turquoise. Continue along the wall, positioning the stencil beside the previous motif so that the spaces are equal.

OPPOSITE: *Make a matching patchwork cushion cover with pieces of fabric stencilled with gold fabric paint. Add offcuts of velvet and cover all the seams with ornate trimmings.*

GEOMETRIC FLOOR TILES

This repeating pattern is derived from an ancient Greek mosaic floor. Cork floor tiles take colour well – only use a small amount of paint and build it up in layers if necessary. Make two stencils, one for each colour, so that the colours do not get mixed.

You will need

- graph paper
- ruler
- pencil
- pair of compasses
- stencil card (stock)
- craft knife and self-healing cutting mat
- masking tape
- 30cm/12in cork tiles
- spray adhesive
- stencil paint in terracotta and blue
- stencil brushes
- acrylic sealer

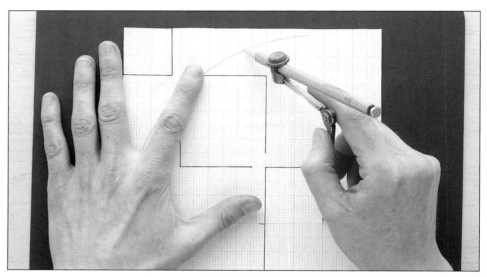

1 Enlarge the quarter section template at the back of the book so that it will fit within a 15cm/6in square. Using graph paper will make the design more accurate. Rule the three squares and draw the curves with a pair of compasses. Rub over all the pencil lines on the back with a pencil.

2 Using a craft knife and self-healing cutting mat, cut two 30cm/12in squares from stencil card (stock). Draw four lines, from corner to corner and edge to edge, to divide each card into eight equal segments. For the first stencil, tape the paper face up to one corner of the first card and draw around the corner and centre square to transfer the design. Repeat on each corner, turning the paper 90 degrees each time. Cut out the five squares. For the second stencil, draw along the curves and around the remaining square. Cut out these eight shapes.

3 Wipe the tile to remove any cork dust. Coat the back of the first stencil with spray adhesive. Stencil the squares using terracotta stencil paint and a stencil brush.

4 Leave to dry, then use the second stencil and blue stencil paint to complete the design. Stencil the remaining tiles in the same way. If you wish, stencil half the tiles in different colours (see below).

5 When all the tiles have been stencilled, spray them with acrylic sealer to make them waterproof. Fix them to the floor following the manufacturer's instructions.

ABOVE: Stencil half the tiles in different colours to make a chequerboard-patterned design on the floor.

ABOVE: A gentle shading of blue has been added to the terracotta shapes and terracotta has been added to the blue shapes to give a softer outline to the strong geometric design.

ABOVE: Experiment with other colours to suit your decor. Different colour combinations create quite different effects. When using more than two colours, you will need to cut more stencils. Alternatively, mask out the area that is to be stencilled in a different colour.

ORGANZA CUSHION

If you always thought stencilling had a simple country look, then think again. This brilliant organza cushion with gold stencilling takes the craft into the luxury class. Use the sharpest dressmaker's pins when handling organza to avoid marking the fabric.

You will need

- dressmaker's graph paper
- ruler
- pencil
- scissors
- dressmaker's pins
- organza, 1m/1⅛yd each in main colour and contrast colour
- stencil card (stock)
- craft knife and self-healing cutting mat
- spray adhesive
- masking tape
- scrap paper
- spray paint in gold
- needle and thread
- sewing machine
- iron
- 50cm/20in cushion pad

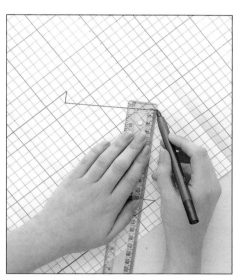

1 Copy the border template at the back of the book on to dressmaker's graph paper and cut it out with scissors. In addition, cut out a 53cm/21in square and a 53 × 40cm/21 × 16in rectangle from graph paper.

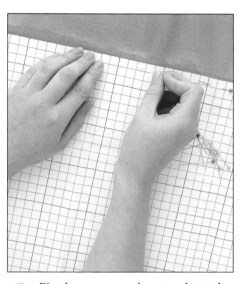

2 Pin the square and rectangle to the main colour of organza. Cut two 53cm/21in squares, and two rectangles measuring 53 × 40cm/21 × 16in. Cut four border pieces from the contrasting colour of organza.

3 Cut a piece of stencil card (stock) 18 × 53cm/7 × 21in. Trace the template and transfer to the card, 8cm/3in from the bottom edge and with 6cm/2½in to spare at each end. Cut out the stencil.

4 Spray the back of the stencil with adhesive and position it along the edge of one organza square. Cut two 45 degree mitres from stencil card, spray with adhesive and press in place. Mask off the surrounding areas with scrap paper.

5 Spray with gold paint. Leave to dry and spray again. Remove the masking paper and stencil. Place the stencil along the next edge, put the mitres in place and continue as before. Stencil the remaining two sides. Hem one long edge of each fabric rectangle by folding over 1cm/³⁄₈in, then 1.5cm/⁵⁄₈in. Pin, tack (baste) and machine stitch the hem, then press.

6 Lay the stencilled fabric square face down and the second square on top. Lay the two rectangles on top, overlapping the stitched edges so that the raw edges line up with the squares. Pin, tack and machine stitch 1cm/³⁄₈in from the raw edge. Trim the seam allowance to 7mm/¹⁄₄in. Pin, tack and stitch the border pieces together at the mitred corners 1.3cm/¹⁄₂in from the raw edges. Trim the corners and turn the right way out. Press. Continue until the border pieces make a ring.

7 Press one of the raw edges under by 1.3cm/¹⁄₂in. Lay the pressed edge of the border fabric along the edge of the main fabric square and pin, tack and machine stitch in place.

8 Turn the cushion over and pull the border over. Turn under the border's raw edge by 1.3cm/¹⁄₂in and pin in place along the front of the cushion. Tack and machine stitch in place. Press. Insert the cushion pad.

TABLECLOTH AND NAPKINS

Inspiration for stencil designs can be all around you, waiting to be discovered. Cutlery and kitchen utensils are wonderful graphic shapes, ideal for stencilling. Arrange them as borders around the edge of a tablecloth and matching napkins or place the knives and forks formally on each side of imaginary place settings.

You will need

- acetate
- craft knife and self-healing cutting mat
- plain-coloured cotton napkins and tablecloth
- fabric paints in various colours
- stencil brush
- fine artist's paintbrush
- medium artist's paintbrush (optional)
- iron

1 Trace the cutlery, heart and utensils templates at the back of the book and cut the stencils from acetate. Lay one of the napkins on a flat surface. Plan your design and start to stencil the cutlery around the edge.

2 Stencil hearts in between the cutlery stencils. Using a fine artist's paintbrush, paint small dots around the hem of the napkins. Use different colours of fabric paint.

3 Using the stencil brush again, stencil hearts on the handles of some of the cutlery.

4 Stencil each napkin with a different pattern, varying the arrangement of the stencils and the colours.

5 Lay the tablecloth on a flat surface and begin to stencil a border of cutlery and hearts.

6 Stencil the larger utensil shapes in the middle of the tablecloth. Stencil the handles first. Stencil the top of the utensils, for example the whisk, in a contrasting colour.

7 Stencil the draining spoons and then add the draining holes in a different colour. Use a medium artist's paintbrush if you prefer to paint the holes.

8 Fill in the blank areas around the utensils with more cutlery stencils. Leave the fabric paint to dry and then iron the reverse of the fabric to fix the paint. Fabric paints are washable so you will have no trouble laundering the tablecloth and napkins.

THROUGH THE GRAPEVINE

This classic grape stencil will bring back holiday memories of sipping wine under a canopy of vines. The stencilled grapes are all the more effective set against the purple and green dry-brushed walls. Practise your paint effects on small pieces of board before tackling full-scale walls.

You will need

- large decorator's paintbrush
- emulsion (latex) paint in purple and green
- pencil
- ruler
- spirit level
- acetate
- craft knife and self-healing cutting mat
- masking tape
- stencil paint in purple and lilac
- stencil brush
- silver gilt cream
- soft cotton cloth

1 Dip the end of a large paintbrush in purple emulsion (latex), scrape off the excess and apply to the wall, brushing in varying directions and not completely covering the wall. This process is known as dry-brushing.

2 Repeat the dry-brushing process with green emulsion, filling in some of the bare areas and going over the purple paint.

3 Draw a horizontal pencil line at the desired height on the wall using a ruler and spirit level.

ROPE AND SHELLS

The chunky rope cleverly linking the seashells is echoed by individual stencilled knots. Shells are always popular motifs for a bathroom design and look good in many colour combinations, from nautical blue and white to greens and aquas or pinks and corals.

You will need

- large household sponges
- emulsion (latex) paint in nautical blue and white
- ruler
- spirit level
- pencil
- acetate
- craft knife and self-healing cutting mat
- masking tape
- stencil paint in dark blue, light blue and camel
- stencil brush
- eraser
- clean cotton cloth

1 Using a household sponge rub nautical blue emulsion (latex) paint over the wall to create a very rough and patchy finish. Leave to dry.

2 Using a clean sponge, rub a generous amount of white emulsion over the wall so that it almost covers the blue, giving a slightly mottled effect.

3 Using a ruler and spirit level, draw a horizontal pencil line at the desired height of the border. Trace the templates at the back of the book and cut the stencils from acetate. Position the seashore stencil with its top edge on the pencil line and secure with masking tape. Stencil dark blue stencil paint around the edges of the shells and seaweed, using a stencil brush.

4 Using light blue stencil paint, shade in the centre of the shells, the seaweed and the recesses of the rope.

5 Using camel stencil paint, fill in the remainder of the rope and then lightly highlight the shells and seaweed. Continue to stencil the shell and rope border right around the room.

6 Draw a vertical line from each loop of rope to the skirting (base) board. Starting 30cm/12in from the stencilled border, make pencil marks at 30cm/ 12in intervals down the line to mark the positions of the rope knots. Start every alternate line of marks 15cm/6in below the border so that the knots will be staggered.

8 Stencil the remainder of the rope in camel. Leave to dry. Remove any visible pencil marks with an eraser and wipe over with a slightly damp cloth.

7 Tape the knotted rope stencil on to the first pencil mark. Stencil dark blue stencil paint in the recesses of the rope.

LEFT: *Create a variation on the sea theme by stencilling a simple row of starfish at dado (chair) rail height. The starfish motif is repeated on the chair seat to give a pleasing coordinated look.*

HERALDIC DINING ROOM

L end an atmosphere of medieval luxury to your dining room with richly coloured walls and heraldic motifs stencilled in the same deep tones. Gilt accessories, heavy fabrics and a profusion of candles team well with this decor. All that remains is to prepare a sumptuous banquet.

You will need

- large household sponges
- emulsion (latex) paint in camel, deep red and deep purple
- ruler
- spirit level
- pencil
- masking tape
- acetate
- craft knife and self-healing cutting mat
- stencil brush
- fine lining brush

1 Using a large household sponge, rub camel emulsion (latex) all over the wall. Leave to dry.

2 Repeat using a generous amount of deep red emulsion so that it almost covers the camel, giving a slightly mottled effect. Leave to dry.

3 Using a ruler and spirit level, draw a pencil line at dado (chair) rail height. Stick a line of masking tape just above it.

4 Sponge deep purple emulsion all over the wall below the masking tape to give a slightly mottled effect. Leave to dry, then remove the masking tape.

5 Trace the heraldic templates at the back of the book and cut the stencils from acetate. Secure the rose stencil above the dividing line with strips of masking tape. Stencil in purple emulsion, using the stencil brush. When dry, position the fleur-de-lys stencil next to the rose and stencil in camel emulsion. Continue to alternate the stencils around the room.

6 Place the highlight stencils over the painted motifs and, with a stencil brush, add purple details to the camel fleurs-de-lys and camel details to the purple roses as shown.

7 Flip the stencils over and position as mirror images below the previously stencilled motifs. Stencil the roses in camel, and the fleurs-de-lys in red.

8 Add highlights as before, using camel on the red fleurs-de-lys, and purple on the camel roses.

9 Using a fine lining brush and camel paint, paint a narrow line where the red and purple paints meet. If you do not have the confidence to do this freehand, position two rows of masking tape on the wall, leaving a small gap in between. When the line of paint is dry, carefully remove the masking tape.

TROMPE L'OEIL PLATES

Ashelf full of trompe l'oeil stencilled plates adds a witty touch to a kitchen wall. Follow this plate design or translate your own patterned china into stencils to give a coordinated look. You could add some individual plates to the wall as well.

You will need

- stencil card (stock)
- pencil
- ruler
- craft knife and self-healing cutting mat
- 23cm/9in diameter plates
- pair of compasses
- spray adhesive
- newspaper or brown paper
- masking tape
- spray paint in white, cream, a range of pinks and mauves, light green, dark green, red, blue and grey

1 Cut three pieces of stencil card (stock) 30cm/12in square. Mark the centre by measuring the centre of each edge and ruling a horizontal and a vertical line across each card to join the marks.

2 Draw a line 3.5cm/1¼in in from all four edges of each card. Place the plate in the centre and draw around the edge. Cut out the plate shape from the first piece of stencil card. This will be stencil 1.

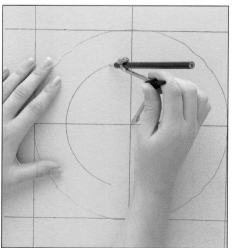

3 Using a pair of compasses, draw a circle about 4cm/1½in from the edge of the plate on the two remaining pieces of card.

4 Trace or photocopy the plate template at the back of the book to the desired size and transfer to the second stencil card.

5 Cut out the design with a craft knife on a self-healing cutting mat. Cut out the smaller areas first and the larger ones last. This will be stencil 2. On the third piece of stencil card, cut out the inner circle. This will be stencil 3.

6 Draw a faint horizontal pencil line on the wall above a shelf. Add two marks 30cm/12in apart on the line to act as a guide for positioning the stencils. Spray the back of the plate stencil (1) with adhesive and place in position on the wall. Press down firmly to ensure a good contact. Mask off the surrounding area with paper and masking tape, leaving no gaps. Spray white and cream spray paint on to the stencil. Remove the masks and stencil.

7 Attach the flower stencil (2) to the wall with spray adhesive, lining it up with the marks on the wall. Mask off the surrounding area. Stick small pieces of masking tape over the leaves on the stencil. Spray the flowers with pinks and mauves, applying a fine layer of paint in short sharp puffs. Try each paint colour on the mask surrounding the stencil first to test the colour and to make sure that the nozzle is clear.

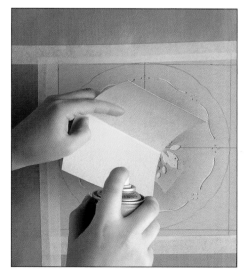

8 Remove the masking tape from the leaves. Fold a small piece of card in half and use it to shield the rest of the stencil from paint. Spray the leaves using light and dark green paints. Take care to avoid spraying paint over the flowers.

9 Cut a small hole in a piece of card and use to spray the centres of the flowers green. Use light green or dark green paint, or vary the two colours.

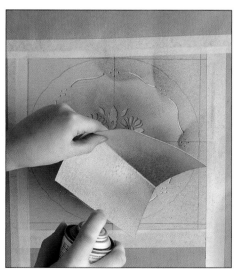

10 Hold the card shield around the dot designs on the border, and spray each one with red paint. Spray blue paint over the wavy lines on the border. Again, do not apply too much paint. Remove the masks and carefully remove the stencil.

11 Spray the back of the last stencil (3) with adhesive and position it on the wall. Mask off the surrounding area as before. Spray an extremely fine mist of grey paint over the top left-hand side and bottom right-hand side of the plate design to create a shadow. Aim the nozzle slightly away from the stencil to ensure that hardly any paint hits the wall. Remove the masks and stencil.

12 Reposition stencil 1 on the wall and spray a very fine mist of blue paint around the edge of the plate. Repeat for the other plates, spacing them evenly along the shelf.

CELESTIAL CHERUBS

This exuberant baroque decoration is perfect for a sumptuous bedroom. The cherubs are stencilled in metallic shades of bronze, gold and copper, but you could use plain colours for a simpler result that would be suitable for a child's room.

You will need

- emulsion (latex) paint in white, blue and grey
- large decorator's paintbrush
- sponge
- stencil card (stock)
- craft knife and self-healing cutting mat
- masking tape
- stencil paint in gold, copper, bronze and white
- stencil brush
- scrap paper

1 Paint the wall with white emulsion (latex). Dilute 1 part blue emulsion with 1 part water, and, using a sponge, lightly apply it to the wall.

2 Sponge in a few areas of grey to give the impression of a cloudy sky. Sponge in a few pale areas by mixing a little white into the grey paint to suggest the edges of clouds.

3 Trace the cherub and heart templates at the back of the book and cut the stencils from stencil card (stock). Secure the cherub stencil to the wall with masking tape. Stencil the body of the cherub in gold stencil paint.

4 Stencil the cherub's wings and bow in copper stencil paint, covering the adjacent parts of the stencil with a piece of scrap paper.

5 Stencil the cherub's hair and arrow in bronze stencil paint, again protecting the adjacent areas with scrap paper.

6 Stencil the drape in white stencil paint. Add some bronze shadows to the folds of the drape.

7 To give a three-dimensional effect to the whole design, add bronze shadows at the edges of various parts of the cherub motif. Follow the shading shown in the photograph below.

8 Stencil more cherubs, varying the design by reversing the card sometimes. Stencil the interlinked hearts in the spaces using bronze stencil paint.

LEFT: Try to position the stencils so that the cupids are aiming their arrows at the interlinked hearts – a perfect theme for a romantic bedroom.

STAMPING

Although stamping is often regarded as a type of stencilling, it is basically a very easy form of printing and produces a very different finished effect. You can make your own stamps from household sponges, or buy commercial stamps in a variety of shapes and sizes. It is a quick and effective technique – all you need is a stamp, a prepared surface and your imagination. As long as the surface is firm enough to take the pressure of the stamp, you can add details to almost anything, from walls to wrapping paper. The best results are achieved by holding the stamp steady and not letting it slide. This will take a little practice, so use a plain sheet of paper first.

ABOVE: Start with a simple, inexpensive project such as stamped wrapping paper and matching gift tags.

LEFT: Here a rose frieze is repeated with single rose motifs on the wall and a single motif on the chair.

STAMPING MATERIALS

Stamps can be constructed from a variety of materials, and a whole range of exciting and stylish effects can be achieved by combining different paints and inks with your chosen stamps.

Dutch metal leaf and gold size

Metal leaf is a cheap, easy-to-use alternative to real gold leaf. Use a sponge stamp to apply gold size in a repeating pattern. When the size is tacky, apply the gold leaf.

Inks

Water-based inks are too runny to use on their own but can be added to wallpaper paste or varnish to make a mixture thick enough to adhere to the stamp. Use them for paper or card (stock), but not for walls. If you are using rubber stamps, inkpads are commercially available in a range of colours.

Interior filler

Add filler, in its dry powdered state, to emulsion (latex) paint to give it body without diluting the colour.

Paint

Water-based paints such as emulsion and artist's acrylics dry quickly to a permanent finish. Use emulsion paint straight from the can or dilute it with wallpaper paste or varnish. For wall treatments, emulsion paint can be thinned with water and sponged or brushed over the wall as a colourwash.

Pre-cut stamps

Rubber stamps are widely available in thousands of designs. Finely detailed motifs are best suited to small-scale projects, while bolder shapes are best for walls and also furniture.

Sponge or foam

Different types of sponge are characterized by their density. High-density sponge is best for detailed shapes and will give a smooth, sharp print. Medium-density sponge or low-density sponge will absorb more paint and give a more textured result.

Varnish

Use water-based acrylic varnish (sold as quick-drying) for stamping projects. It can be mixed with emulsion paint or ink to thicken the texture and create a range of different sheens. The varnish will also protect and preserve the design of your stamp.

Wallpaper paste

This allows you to thin emulsion paint without making it too runny to adhere to the stamp. Mix up the paste with the required amount of water first, then add the emulsion.

RIGHT: 1 Dutch metal leaf and gold size, 2 coloured inks, 3 low-density sponge, 4 pre-cut stamp, 5 high-density sponge, 6 medium-density sponges, 7 interior filler, 8 emulsion (latex) paint, 9 varnish, 10 wallpaper paste.

STAMPING EQUIPMENT

Stamping is a very simple craft and does not require a great deal of specialist equipment. Most of the items illustrated here will already be found in an ordinary household.

Craft knife and self-healing cutting mat

A sharp-bladed craft knife is essential for cutting your own stamps out of sponge. Use a self-healing cutting mat to protect your work surface, and always direct the blade away from your fingers.

Linoleum blocks

These are available from art and craft shops and can be cut to make stamps which recreate the look of a wood block. You'll need special linoleum-cutting tools, which are also easily available, to scoop out the areas around the design. Always hold the linoleum with your spare hand behind your cutting hand for safety.

Masking tape

Use for masking off areas of walls and furniture.

Natural sponge

Use for applying colourwashes to walls and other larger surfaces before stamping.

Paintbrushes

A range of decorator's brushes is needed for painting furniture and walls before stamping. Use a broad brush to apply colourwashes to walls. Stiff brushes can be used to stipple paint on to stamps for textured effects, while finer brushes are used to pick out details or to apply paint to the stamp.

Pencils, pens and crayons

Use a soft pencil to trace templates for stamps, and for making easily removable guidelines on walls. Draw motifs freehand using a felt-tipped pen on medium- and low-density sponge. Use a white crayon on black upholstery foam.

Rags

Keep a stock of clean rags and cloths for cleaning stamps and preparing surfaces.

Ruler and tape measure

Use these to plan your design.

Scissors

Use sharp scissors to cut out medium- and low-density sponge shapes and also for cutting out templates.

Sponge rollers

Small paint rollers can be used to load your stamps. You will need several if you are stamping in different colours.

RIGHT: 1 scissors, 2 craft knife,
3 masking tape, 4 paint rollers, 5 ruler,
6 tape measure, 7 pencils, 8 self-healing
cutting mat, 9 rag, 10 natural sponge,
11 paintbrushes.

STAMPING TECHNIQUES

Stamping is a quick and effective method of repeating a design on a wide variety of surfaces, using many different mixtures of paints and inks. Ready-made stamps are widely available, usually mounted on wooden blocks, but they are also easy to make yourself using foam or sponge.

MAKING STAMPS

1 Use high-density sponge to create sharply defined and detailed designs. Trace your chosen motif using a soft pencil to give dark, clear lines.

2 Roughly cut around the design, then spray the piece of tracing paper with adhesive to hold it in place on the sponge while you are cutting it out.

3 Cut along the outline of the motif using a craft knife, then, pinching the background sections, cut them away holding the blade away from your fingers.

4 The surface of low-density sponge is too soft to use tracing paper as a guide for cutting out the stamp. It is easier to draw the design straight on to the sponge using a felt-tipped pen.

5 Sharp scissors can be used to cut out stamps made from low-density sponge and they are especially useful for cutting out the basic shapes of the motif.

6 As with high-density sponge, the unwanted background areas should be cut away with a craft knife when the outline has been cut, but care is needed as this sponge will tear more easily. Rinse the completed stamp to remove the remains of the felt-tipped pen ink.

PAINT MIXTURES

Wallpaper paste and emulsion paint

Add 50 per cent paste to the emulsion (latex) paint to give a watercolour effect without producing a mixture that is too runny to work with. Apply the mixture using a roller, sponge or paintbrush, or dip the stamp into the paint on a flat plate.

Wallpaper paste and ink

Wallpaper paste thickens the texture of ink, while keeping the rich colour. The effect produced depends on the proportion of ink in the mixture. It will give a more even spread of colour than using emulsion (latex). Apply using a roller or paintbrush.

Varnish and emulsion paint

The density of the emulsion (latex) paint is diluted as with wallpaper paste, but this can also be used to create different sheens according to the type of varnish used. Apply with a roller, paintbrush or sponge, or dip the stamp into the paint on a plate.

Varnish and ink

This effect is similar to the wallpaper paste mixture, but creates a smoother mix as both materials are fine in texture. Again, different sheens can be obtained depending on the varnish used. Apply with a roller.

Wallpaper paste and woodstain

The wallpaper paste dilutes the colour density of the woodstain while thickening the mixture for ease of use. Use quick-drying, water-based woodstains, which are available in a range of colours. Apply with a roller.

Interior filler and emulsion paint

This mixture thickens the paint as opposed to diluting the colour, and is good for creating relief effects. Apply the mixture generously, using a paintbrush, or dip the stamp into the paint on a plate.

HOW TO APPLY PAINT

Using a roller

Pour a little paint on to the side of a flat plate, then, using a small sponge roller, pick up a small amount of paint and roll it out over the rest of the plate until you have an even covering. Roll the paint on to the stamp.

Using a paintbrush

Use a fairly stiff brush and apply the paint with a dabbing or stippling motion. This technique enables more than one colour to be applied and for detail to be picked out. Be careful not to overload the stamp, as this may cause it to slip when stamping.

Dipping into paint on a plate

Brush a thin coat of paint on to a flat plate, then press the stamp into the paint. You may need to do this several times to get an even coating. Initially the stamp will absorb a good amount of paint. Keep brushing more paint on to the plate as you work.

Using a roller and brush

Use a sponge roller to apply the paint evenly over the whole stamp. Use a brush to apply a second colour to act as a highlight or shadow, or to pick out details of the design.

Using a sponge

Spread an even coating of paint on a plate, then use a natural sponge to pick up the paint and dab it on to the stamp. This method allows you to put a light, even covering of paint on to the stamp.

Using an inkpad

Press the stamp lightly on to the inkpad. You may need to do this several times to ensure a good covering. It is difficult to overload the stamp using inkpads. This technique will give a dry look to the stamped motifs.

PREPARING SURFACES

Tiles, china and glass

These are all prepared in the same way, using soapy water to remove dirt and grease, then drying with a lint-free cloth. Appropriate special paints, such as enamel or ceramic paints, must be used as normal emulsion (latex) and acrylic paints will not adhere well and are not sufficiently durable for these surfaces. It is often necessary to strengthen the finished design by applying a coat of varnish.

1 Wash the tile or glass with soapy water and rinse thoroughly. To remove any remaining traces of grease, give the surface a final wipe with a cloth dipped in methylated spirits (methyl alcohol) and leave to dry.

2 When printing on a curved surface, carefully roll the stamp while holding the object securely. Sponge stamps are best suited for this purpose. Rubber stamps are less suitable.

Fabrics

Fabrics must be washed and ironed before stamping to remove any dressing and allow for any shrinkage. Use special fabric paint or ink so that the item can be washed after stamping. Fix the paint to the fabric according to the manufacturer's instructions.

1 Once ironed, lay the fabric on a flat surface and tape down the edges to hold it firmly in position.

2 Place a piece of card (stock) or scrap paper under the area to be stamped to stop any of the paint bleeding through the fabric.

Wood

Wood should be lightly sanded before stamping and varnished afterwards. New wood should be sealed with a coat of shellac to stop resin leaking through the grain. When using woodstains, keep the stamp quite dry to stop the stain bleeding into the grain of the wood.

1 Sand the surface of the wood, then wipe down with a soft cloth to remove any loose dust.

2 Once dry, the stamped design can be rubbed back with abrasive paper to create a distressed effect.

PLANNING A DESIGN

1 With the aid of a spirit level, draw a faint pencil line to use as a guide when stamping.

2 Stamp the motif several times on scrap paper and cut out the prints. Tape them to the wall so that you can judge how your design will look.

3 When using a stamp mounted on a block, you can draw a straight line on the back to help with positioning. Align the block with the pencil guideline on the wall.

4 A piece of card (stock) held between the previous print and the stamp will ensure that there is consistent spacing between the motifs.

5 For a tighter design, butt the stamped motifs together without any spacing.

6 Once the paint is dry, the pencil guideline can be removed using a clean cloth wrung out in soapy water and rubbed along the line.

STAMP EFFECTS

Although basic stamping is a very simple and straightforward technique, you can achieve many different and subtle effects with stamps, depending on the paint mixture you use and the way in which it is applied. The same stamp, cut from high-density sponge, was used to make all the following prints.

Half-shade

Roll the first, paler colour over the stamp, then roll a second, darker shade over one half only, to create a three-dimensional shadowed effect.

Two-tone

Using a paintbrush, load the stamp with the first colour, then apply the second colour to the top and bottom edges only.

Two-tone with dry roller

For an even subtler colour mix, roll the second colour right over the first using a very dry roller.

Contrasting detail

To pick out details of the design in a contrasting colour, apply the first colour with a roller, then use a paintbrush to apply the second contrasting colour in the areas you want.

Partial outline

This shadow effect is produced by stamping the motif in one colour, then partially outlining the print using a paintbrush or felt-tip pen. For a natural shadow effect, place all the shadow on either the right-hand or left-hand side.

Drop shadow

Another, very subtle, effect of shadows and highlights can be produced by stamping the motif in the darker colour first. When this is dry, load the stamp with the paler colour and print over the first image, positioning the stamp slightly to one side.

Stippled

This stippled effect gives the stamped print lots of surface interest. Apply the paint with a stiff paintbrush and a dabbing, stippling motion.

Wallpaper paste

Adding wallpaper paste to emulsion (latex) paint gives the stamped print a translucent, watercolour quality.

Light shadow

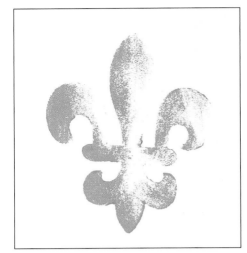

Here the paint has been applied with a roller, covering each element of the motif more heavily on one side to create a delicate shadow effect.

Second print

After loading the stamp with paint, print first on a piece of scrap paper. This very delicate image is the second print.

Sponge print

Apply a sponge print in one colour over a rollered colour in another colour for a different effect, as shown here.

Distressed

A single colour of paint applied with a dry roller produces an aged, distressed paint effect.

STRAWBERRY FRUIT BASKET

Strawberry motifs always look fresh and pretty, with their bright red fruits and shapely leaves, and the sponging technique used here suits the texture of strawberries particularly well. This decorative planter would look lovely on a kitchen windowsill filled with herbs or, of course, with strawberry plants.

You will need

- medium-grade abrasive paper
- wooden planter
- medium decorator's paintbrush
- matt emulsion (flat latex) paint in white
- medium-density sponge, such as a kitchen sponge
- felt-tipped pen
- scissors or craft knife and cutting mat
- pencil
- acrylic paint in red, green and yellow
- fine artist's paintbrush
- clear acrylic varnish and brush

1 Lightly sand the planter with medium-grade abrasive paper to prepare the surface for painting.

2 Apply two coats of white emulsion (latex) paint, allowing the paint to dry and sanding lightly between coats.

3 Copy the strawberry, leaf and calyx templates from the back of the book. Draw around them on the sponge with a felt-tipped pen. Cut away the sponge around the shapes using scissors or a craft knife and cutting mat.

4 Mark the positions of the strawberries on the planter in pencil. Load the strawberry stamp with red acrylic paint, then stamp the strawberries on the planter. Allow to dry.

5 Load the calyx stamp with green acrylic paint and stamp a calyx just above each strawberry shape.

6 Mark the positions of the large and small leaves on the planter. Load the leaf stamp with green paint and stamp the leaves, making the large leaves by stamping three times.

8 Use the fine artist's paintbrush to paint yellow seeds on the strawberries. When the paint is dry, apply two coats of clear acrylic varnish, all over the planter to protect the design.

7 Allow the leaves to dry, then use a pencil to mark the positions of the stems. Paint the stems freehand using a fine artist's paintbrush and green paint.

FLOWER POT FRIEZE

This witty frieze has a 1950s feel and creates an eye-catching feature above a half-boarded wall. Use scraps of left-over wallpaper or sheets of wrapping paper for the pots, then stamp an exuberant display of flowers to go inside them.

You will need

- matt emulsion (flat latex) paint in pale blue and white
- 2 large decorator's paintbrushes
- clean cotton cloth
- pencil
- wallpaper or wrapping paper
- scissors
- PVA (white) glue and brush
- acrylic paint in green
- fine artist's paintbrush
- stamp inkpads in a variety of colours
- large and small daisy rubber stamps
- cotton wool buds (swabs)
- scrap paper

1 Paint the tongue-and-groove boarding or the lower half of the wall with pale blue emulsion (latex) paint. Leave to dry.

2 Using a dry paintbrush, lightly brush white emulsion over the flat colour. For a softer effect, rub the paint in with a cotton cloth.

3 To make the frieze, draw flower-pot shapes on to scraps of different wallpapers or wrapping paper and cut them out. Cut scalloped strips of paper and glue one along the top of each flower pot, using PVA (white) glue.

4 Glue the flower pots along the wall, at evenly spaced intervals. Alternate the different papers to create a pleasing random effect.

5 Using acrylic paint and a fine artist's paintbrush, paint green stems coming out of each pot. Leave the paint to dry before beginning to print the flowers.

6 Use coloured inkpads to ink the daisy stamps, using the lighter colours first. To ink the flower centre in a different colour, remove the first colour from the centre using a cottonwool bud (swab), then use a small inkpad to dab on the second colour.

7 Test the daisy stamps on a sheet of scrap paper before applying them to the wall.

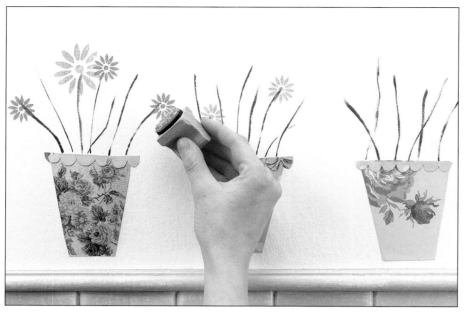

8 Print the lighter-coloured flowers on the ends of some of the stems, using both the large and small daisy stamps. Allow the ink to dry.

9 Print darker flowers on the remaining stems. Allow the flowers to overlap to create full, blossoming pots.

GRAPEVINE FRIEZE AND GLASSES

This elegant repeating design is a combination of sponging and freehand painting – practise the strokes on paper before embarking on the wall, and keep your hand relaxed to make confident, sweeping lines. It's perfect for a kitchen or conservatory and is repeated on a set of glasses to carry the theme on to the table.

You will need

- medium-density sponge
- felt-tipped pen
- small coin
- scissors or craft knife and self-healing cutting mat
- ruler
- pencil
- acrylic paint in shades of purple and blue
- paint-mixing container
- medium and fine artist's paintbrushes
- glasses
- kitchen cloth
- ceramic paint in purple and blue

1 Copy the template at the back of the book and use to draw the leaf shape on a piece of medium-density sponge. To make the stamp for the grapes, draw around a small coin, or copy the grape template.

2 Cut out the sponge shapes using a pair of scissors or a craft knife and self-healing cutting mat.

3 Trace the template of the frieze design on to the wall where you want it to appear, carefully marking the positions of the grapes and leaves.

4 Mix together two shades of purple acrylic paint. Using a medium artist's paintbrush, load one side of the grape stamp with dark purple paint and the other with a lighter shade to give a shadowed effect.

5 Build up the bunch of grapes, starting with the top row and working downwards to avoid smudges. Position the grapes in succeeding rows diagonally between the ones above, as shown. Keep the dark side of each grape facing the same way.

6 Mix two shades of blue paint and load the leaf stamp, painting the outside edge in the darker shade. Stamp the leaf shape where marked on either side of each bunch of grapes. Paint the stems freehand in the lighter shade of blue, using a fine brush.

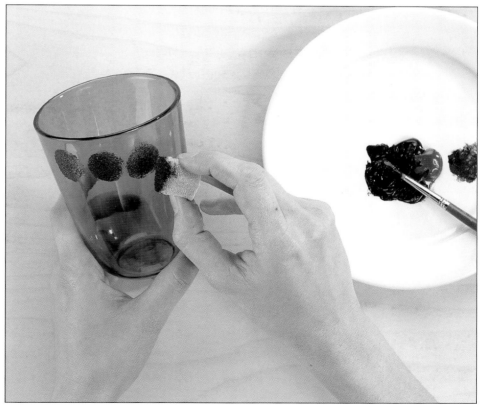

7 Before decorating the glasses with the grape motif, clean each thoroughly to remove any trace of grease. Leave to dry.

8 Mix two shades of purple ceramic paint and load the grape stamp as before, with dark purple on one side and a lighter shade on the other. Align the first row of grapes below the edge of the glass, keeping clear of the rim.

9 Continue to build up the bunch of grapes until it fills one side of the glass. Keep the dark side of each grape facing the same way.

10 Mix two shades of blue ceramic paint and load the leaf stamp as before. Stamp a leaf motif on either side of the bunch of grapes.

11 Paint the stems in the lighter shade of blue, using a fine brush. Leave the glass for 24 hours to dry completely. The glasses will withstand gentle washing but should not be put in a dishwasher or cleaned with an abrasive scourer.

SPOTTED FLOWER POTS

Customized terracotta pots will give a new, fresh look to your conservatory, patio or kitchen windowsill. Light, bright colours suit this project really well, but you can make them as subtle or as bold as you please. The end of a small sponge roller gives a neat, sharp image for the spot motifs.

You will need

- terracotta flower pots
- white acrylic primer
- medium decorator's paintbrushes
- matt emulsion (flat latex) paint in a variety of colours including yellow, white, red and blue
- paint-mixing container
- old plate
- small sponge paint rollers
- satin acrylic varnish and brush

1 Make sure the flower pots are clean and dry. Prime them with a coat of white acrylic primer and leave to dry.

2 Dilute some yellow emulsion (latex) paint with water to the consistency of single (light) cream. Colourwash the first pot using a dry brush and random brushstrokes. Allow to dry.

3 Spread some white paint on to an old plate. Press the end of a small sponge paint roller into the paint, then press it firmly on to the first flower pot. Remove carefully and repeat all over the pot. Leave to dry.

4 Repeat using red paint over half the white spots, but position the sponge slightly to one side of each white spot to give a highlighted three-dimensional effect. Colour the rest of the spots blue. Leave to dry.

5 Repeat on the other flower pots, using different colour combinations. Seal the pots with two to three thin, even coats of satin acrylic varnish, allowing the varnish to dry between coats.

HERB BOX

A miniature chest of drawers with decorations on a botanical theme makes a charming store for dried herbs in the pantry, or would look equally good in the potting shed, filled with seeds. Small, unpainted wooden chests are inexpensive and widely available.

You will need

- unpainted wooden chest of drawers
- 6 unpainted wooden knobs with screws
- acrylic primer in white
- medium decorator's paintbrushes
- matt emulsion (flat latex) paint in pale green and very pale green
- clear wax and brush
- medium-grade abrasive paper
- ruler
- pencil
- drill and drill bit
- rubber stamps in plant designs
- stamp inkpad in green
- screwdriver

1 Prime the chest, drawers and knobs with an even coat of white acrylic primer. Allow to dry. If the drawers have thumb-holes in their fronts, as here, reverse them when you replace the drawers later.

2 Paint the chest, drawers and knobs with pale green emulsion (latex). Leave to dry thoroughly.

3 Apply clear wax to the edges and corners, wherever the chest and knobs would receive most natural wear and tear. Allow to set for 10 minutes.

4 Using the decorator's paintbrush, paint on a coat of very pale green emulsion and allow to dry.

5 Using medium-grade abrasive paper, rub down the areas where the wax was applied to reveal the base colour.

6 Mark each drawer 2.5cm/1in down from the centre top in pencil and drill a hole for the knob.

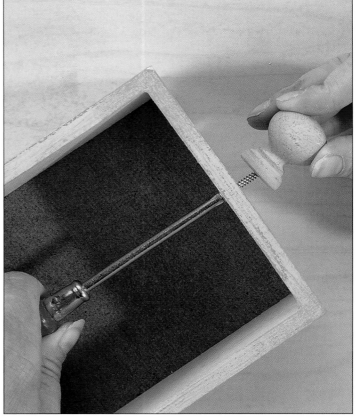

7 Ink a rubber stamp using the green inkpad and press on to the drawer below the drilled hole. Choose a different herb or flower design for each drawer.

8 When the stamped designs are dry, screw the knobs to the drawers. Place the drawers back in the chest.

SUN-STAR BLIND

Turn a plain white blind into a chic window dressing by colourwashing it to give a pretty, cloudy effect, then adding a vibrant pattern of stamped motifs. Fix on an ornate blind-pull or tassel to give the finishing touch.

You will need

- matt emulsion (flat latex) paint in purple and yellow
- acrylic scumble glaze
- paint-mixing container
- plain white roller blind
- natural sponge
- black and gold felt-tipped pens
- paper
- scissors
- 12.5cm/5in square of high-density sponge, such as upholstery foam
- craft knife and self-healing cutting mat
- old plate
- bradawl or awl
- brass screw eye
- blind-pull or tassel

1 Mix some purple emulsion (latex) paint with acrylic scumble glaze. Lay the blind on a flat surface. Dip a natural sponge into the paint and wipe the colour over the blind in a circular motion to give a soft, cloudy effect. Allow to dry.

2 Draw the sun-star design freehand on a piece of paper and cut it out. Trace around the shape on to a square of high-density sponge. Cut out using a craft knife and self-healing cutting mat.

3 Spread some yellow emulsion paint
on to an old plate. Press the sun-
star sponge shape on to the paint,
ensuring the surface is entirely covered,
then on to the blind. Repeat, spacing the
sun-stars evenly and overlapping the
edges of the blind. Allow to dry.

4 Outline each sun-star shape using a
gold felt-tipped pen. Add a small
circle in the centre.

5 Make a hole in the centre of the
bottom batten using a bradawl or
awl and screw in a small brass eye.
Attach a decorative blind-pull or tassel.

MOORISH TILE EFFECT

Moorish wall patterns are based on abstract, geometric motifs which you can reproduce most effectively with stamps. In this wall treatment, a lozenge shape is incorporated in a subtle tile design on a cool colourwashed background.

You will need

- matt emulsion (flat latex) paint in mid-blue, off-white and terracotta
- wallpaper paste
- paint-mixing container
- Large and small decorator's paintbrushes
- thin card (stock)
- ruler
- pencil
- scissors
- medium-density sponge, such as a kitchen sponge
- felt-tipped pen
- craft knife
- spirit level
- fine artist's paintbrush

1 Mix the mid-blue emulsion (latex) with 50 per cent wallpaper paste. Apply to the walls with a large paintbrush, working at random angles and blending the brushstrokes to avoid any hard edges.

2 Mix the off-white emulsion with 75 per cent wallpaper paste and brush on to the walls as before, to soften the effect. Allow to dry.

3 To make a template for the tile shape, cut out a 30cm/12in square of thin card (stock).

4 Mark the sides of the card square 5cm/2in from each corner, draw a line across the diagonal and cut off the corners.

5 Copy the template from the back of the book and transfer it to a 5cm/ 2in square of medium-density sponge using a felt-tipped pen. Cut away the excess sponge using a craft knife.

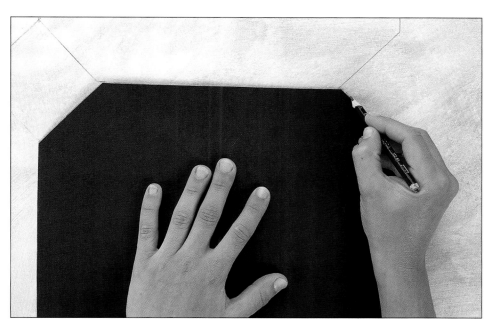

6 Using a spirit level, draw a horizontal line around the room where you want the top of the pattern. Place the top of the card template against the line and draw around it. Repeat all over the pattern area.

7 Use small decorator's paintbrushes to load the stamp with mid-blue and terracotta emulsion paint. Print the motif in the diamond shapes created by the template.

8 Dilute off-white emulsion with water to the consistency of thick cream. Using a fine artist's paintbrush, paint over the pencil lines.

SANTA FE LIVING ROOM

Aztec motifs such as this bird are bold, stylized and one-dimensional, and translate perfectly into stamps. Strong colour contrasts suit this style, but here the pattern is confined to widely spaced stripes over a cool white wall, and further restrained with a final light wash of white paint.

You will need

- matt emulsion (flat latex) paint in off-white, warm white, deep red and navy blue
- paint-mixing container
- natural sponge
- large and medium decorator's paintbrushes
- plumbline
- ruler
- pencil
- masking tape
- felt-tipped pen
- medium-density sponge, such as a household sponge
- craft knife
- small paint roller
- old plate
- high-density sponge, such as upholstery foam

1 Dilute the off-white emulsion (latex) paint with 50 per cent water and apply a wash over the walls using a sponge, alternating the angle at which you work. Allow to dry.

2 Using a large, dry brush, apply warm white emulsion to some areas to achieve a rough-looking surface. Allow to dry.

3 Starting 10cm/4in from one corner, and using a plumbline as a guide, draw a straight pencil line from the top to the bottom of the wall.

4 Measure 45cm/18in along the wall, hang the plumbline again and mark a second vertical line. Draw another line 10cm/4in away to create a band. Repeat all around the room.

5 Apply masking tape to the walls on each outer edge of the marked bands.

6 Paint the bands in deep red emulsion using a medium decorator's paintbrush. Leave to dry.

7 Draw a 10 × 20cm/4 × 8in diamond shape on to medium-density sponge. Cut out the shape using a craft knife.

8 Use a small roller to load the stamp with navy blue emulsion paint. Stamp the diamonds down the red bands, starting from the top and just touching at the tips.

9 Copy the bird template at the back of the book on to a piece of high-density sponge. Cut away the excess sponge using a craft knife.

10 Use the small roller to load the bird stamp with off-white emulsion. Print the birds upright, roughly in the centre of the diamonds. Make sure that they all face in the same direction.

11 When the bird motifs are dry, use minimal pressure and a large dry paintbrush to brush gently over each band with warm white emulsion (latex). This will soften the bold colours.

FOLK-ART CHAIR

Simple repeating designs on a white painted chair have a wonderfully naïve charm. Stick to a few bright colours in keeping with the folk-art style of this design, which any slight irregularities in the stamping will only serve to enhance.

You will need

- medium-grade abrasive paper
- wooden chair
- matt emulsion (flat latex) paint in white
- medium decorator's paintbrushes
- medium-density sponge, such as a kitchen sponge
- felt-tipped pen
- coin
- cork from a wine bottle
- craft knife
- pencil
- ruler
- acrylic paint in black, red, terracotta and blue
- paint-mixing container
- scrap paper
- clear acrylic varnish and brush

1 Sand the chair with medium-grade abrasive paper to remove any rough patches or old paint or varnish.

2 Paint the chair with two coats of white emulsion (latex) paint, allowing the paint to dry between coats.

3 Copy the heart and leaf from the back of the book. Draw around the templates on to the sponge using a felt-tipped pen. Draw around a coin on to the end of a cork to make the spot stamp.

4 Cut out the excess sponge around the motifs using a craft knife. Cut out the cork spot motif.

5 Using a pencil and ruler, mark the positions of the leaves, 6cm/2½in apart, on the struts of the chair back and on the seat.

6 Load the leaf stamp with black acrylic paint, then stamp once on a piece of scrap paper to remove excess paint. Stamp along the struts at a 45 degree angle. Alternate the direction of the leaves on each strut.

7 Load the heart stamp with red acrylic paint, remove the excess paint as before and stamp a heart at the top of each vertical strut, across the back and front of the chair.

8 Load the cork with terracotta acrylic paint, remove the excess paint as before and stamp a dot between each leaf shape.

9 Wash the terracotta paint off the cork, load it with blue and stamp dots 2cm/¾in apart along the legs and all round the edge of the chair.

10 Leave the paint to dry, then apply two coats of clear acrylic varnish to protect the design. Allow the varnish to dry between coats.

STAMPED WRAPPING PAPER

Y ou can turn plain sheets of paper into fabulous hand-printed gift wrap using simple, bold linoleum-cut motifs and coloured inks. The designs are finished off using small rubber stamps. For the chequerboard design, position the linoleum block carefully to get an even pattern. Cut up a large sheet to make gift tags, threaded with narrow ribbon.

You will need

- linoleum board
- felt-tipped pen
- wood offcut
- linoleum-cutting tools
- water-soluble printing ink in a variety of colours
- small pane of glass or old saucer
- rubber ink roller
- plain wrapping paper
- metal spoon
- small star and spot rubber stamps
- stamp inkpads in a variety of colours
- hole punch
- narrow ribbon

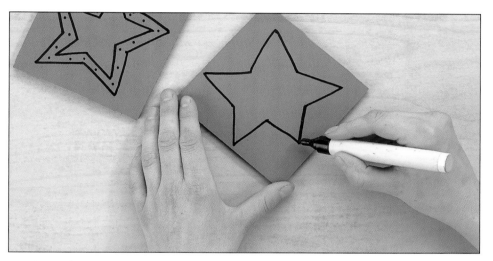

1 Draw the star and star outline freehand on to paper. Cut out and copy on to two squares of linoleum, using a felt-tipped pen.

2 Butt the first linoleum square against an offcut of wood and place the wood against a wall on a flat surface, to prevent the linoleum from slipping. Cut away the area around the design using linoleum-cutting tools.

3 To cut out the spots for the star outline you will need a fine cutting tool. Place the point of the tool on a marked spot and scoop out the linoleum. Dust away the shavings.

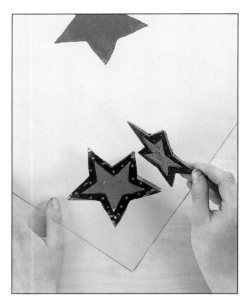

4 Select a coloured ink for the star shape and squeeze a small amount on to a piece of glass or old saucer. Roll out the ink until it feels tacky, then roll it on to the star stamp. Do not apply too much or the linoleum will slip when printing.

5 Position the star stamp on the paper and press down, holding firmly in place. Smooth the back of the linoleum with the back of a metal spoon. Reapply the ink before printing each star.

6 Use a darker shade of ink for the star outline and line it up carefully over the plain shape. Smooth over the back of the linoleum with a metal spoon.

7 To complete the star design, use a small star-shaped rubber stamp and coloured inkpads to match the colours of the large stars. Stamp the small stars at random between the large ones. Repeat the motifs on gift tags, punch a hole with a hole punch and thread with narrow ribbon.

8 Follow the design in the picture to make a chequerboard stamp in the same way. Finish with a small spot-shaped rubber stamp on each square.

ART NOUVEAU ROSES

This stylized, flowing design is inspired by the rose motif found in the work of Charles Rennie Mackintosh, who used it repeatedly in his interior designs, on chairs, doors, leaded glass and textiles. Used here to link a chair with the wall behind it, it is equally effective as a single motif or as a repeating pattern.

You will need

- pencil
- scissors
- high-density sponge, such as upholstery foam
- craft knife and cutting mat
- ruler
- stiff card (stock)
- PVA (white) glue and brush
- felt-tipped pen
- small coin
- medium artist's paintbrush
- acrylic paint in pink and green
- director's chair with calico cover
- tailor's chalk
- fabric paint in green and pink

1 Scale up the designs at the back of the book to the size you require and make templates. Cut a square of sponge to fit the rose and a rectangle for the stem. Cut two pieces of card (stock) to fit the sponge shapes and glue them on using PVA (white) glue.

2 Using a felt-tipped pen, transfer the designs to the sponge by drawing around the templates. Mark the top of each design on the card at the back.

3 Cut away the excess sponge from around the motifs using a craft knife. Make the stamp for the small dots by drawing around a small coin and cutting it out.

4 Using a pencil and ruler, and with the large stamp as a size guide, mark the positions of the bottom edges of the roses and stems on the wall, keeping the line parallel with the dado (chair) rail. Repeat for the upper line of roses, then mark the centres of the small dots directly above the lower ones, and on a line equidistant from the two rows of roses.

5 Using a medium artist's paintbrush, load the rose stamp evenly with a quantity of pink acrylic paint.

6 Match the bottom edge of the stamp to the marked wall and apply the stamp.

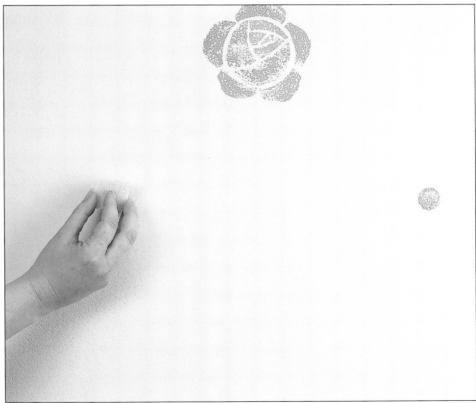

7 Load the small dot stamp with green acrylic paint. Stamp dots at the marked points on the wall.

8 Load the stem stamp with green paint and stamp at the marked points. Repeat to complete the rows.

9 Remove the calico cover from the back of the chair and lay it out flat. Using tailor's chalk, mark the positions for the motifs along a line 5cm/2in in from each side. Load the stem stamp with green fabric paint and position the bottom edge on the marked line.

10 Load the rose stamp with pink fabric paint to complete the stamped design. Leave to dry, then rub off the chalk marks and fix the fabric paints according to the manufacturer's instructions.

PLASTER WALL TREATMENT

Add an extra dimension to stamping by creating a relief effect on your walls. For this technique, a mixture of paint and interior filler (Spackle) is applied to the stamp and then pressed on to the wall, leaving a raised motif. A monochromatic scheme suits this look best.

You will need

- matt emulsion (flat latex) paint in off-white, lime white and stone white
- wallpaper paste
- paint-mixing container
- large and medium decorator's paintbrushes
- 45cm/18in square of card (stock)
- pencil
- high-density sponge, such as upholstery foam
- felt-tipped pen or white crayon
- craft knife
- interior filler (Spackle)

1 Mix the off-white emulsion (latex) with 50 per cent wallpaper paste. Apply to the walls with a large paintbrush, working at random angles and keeping the effect quite rough.

2 Apply random patches of lime white emulsion, allowing the off-white base coat to show in areas.

3 Using the card (stock) square as a template and beginning in a corner of the room, make a small mark at each corner of the card. Reposition the card using the previous marks as a guide and repeat to form a grid of evenly spaced marks around the room.

Copy the template at the back of the book and transfer it to a piece of high-density sponge. Cut away the excess sponge using a craft knife.

5 Using a medium paintbrush, mix stone white emulsion with interior filler (Spackle), using about 1 part filler to 3 parts paint.

6 Apply the mixture thickly to the stamp using a dabbing motion.

7 Print over each pencil mark,
   pressing the stamp quite hard and
pulling it cleanly away – be careful not
to smear the impression. Leave for about
4 hours to dry.

8 Dry brush a little lime white
   emulsion over each stamp, so that
only the areas in highest relief pick up
the paint. Do not attempt to make all
the motifs the same – the charm of this
technique lies in the slight irregularities.

GOTHIC DINING ROOM

Create a dramatic setting for candlelit dinner parties with purple and gold panels that will shimmer from deep velvety green walls. The effect is achieved by stamping the wall or walls with gold size and then rubbing on Dutch gold leaf which will adhere to the stamped motifs.

You will need

- 30cm/12in square of thin card (stock)
- ruler
- pencil
- scissors
- high-density sponge, such as upholstery foam
- felt-tipped pen
- craft knife
- matt emulsion (flat latex) paint in dark green and purple
- natural sponge
- plumbline
- small paint roller
- old plate
- gold size
- Dutch gold leaf
- soft brush

1 To make a template for the wall panels, draw a freehand arc from the centre top of the card (stock) square to the lower corner.

2 Fold the card in half down the centre and cut out both sides to make a symmetrical Gothic arch shape.

3 Copy the design from the back of the book and make a paper pattern with a diameter of 10cm/4in. Transfer the design on to a piece of high-density sponge. Cut away the excess sponge using a craft knife.

4 Apply dark green emulsion (latex) paint liberally to the wall or walls, using a sponge and working in a circular motion. Allow to dry.

5 Using a plumbline as a guide and beginning 23cm/9in from a corner, mark a vertical line up the wall to a height of 1.8m/6ft.

6 Measure across the wall and use the plumbline to draw vertical lines every 60cm/2ft.

7 Measure out 15cm/6in each side of each vertical and draw two more lines to mark the edges of the panels.

8 Place the point of the card template at the centre top point of each panel and draw in the curves.

9 Use a small paint roller to load the stamp with gold size. Print each panel, beginning with the centre top and working down the central line, then down each side.

10 When the size is tacky, apply Dutch gold leaf by rubbing over the backing paper with a soft brush.

11 Once the panel is complete, use the soft brush to remove any excess gold leaf.

12 Using only the centre of the stamp, fill in the spaces between the gold motifs using purple emulsion paint.

INDIAN VELVET CUSHION

Indian textile printing blocks are available in numerous designs. This is an opulent way to decorate cushions or other fabric accessories. Add metallic powders to fabric-painting medium to give a glittery effect with a hardwearing finish.

You will need

- 150cm/1½yd velvet
- tape measure
- scissors
- dressmaker's pins
- sewing machine and matching sewing thread
- 4 gold tassels
- bronze powder
- fabric-painting medium
- paint-mixing container
- medium paintbrush
- scrap paper
- Indian textile printing block
- 3 gold buttons
- sewing needle
- 56cm/22in cushion pad

1 Cut out a 58cm/23in square and two rectangles 33 × 58cm/13 × 23in from the velvet. Turn in, pin and stitch a double hem along one long edge of each rectangle. Make three buttonholes, evenly spaced, in the hem of one piece.

2 Right sides together, pin the button-holed piece to the square front on three sides. Pin the second back piece on top, stitched hems overlapping. Insert a tassel in the seam at each corner, facing in. Stitch and turn through. Flatten the seams and lay the cushion on a flat surface.

3 Add 1 part bronze powder to 2 parts fabric-painting medium and mix. Insert scrap paper inside the cushion to protect the other side. Prime the block with the mixture and position it along one edge of the cushion and press down. Repeat to complete the design.

4 Remove the scrap paper. Sew a gold button opposite each buttonhole on the back of the cushion cover. Insert the cushion pad and fasten the buttons.

SAILING BOAT FRIEZE

Use this charming yacht bobbing on the waves to decorate a bathroom with a nautical theme. It is better, if possible, to stamp tiles before fixing them to the wall, so that the ceramic paints can be made more resilient by baking in the oven. You can stamp and appliqué the same design, with embroidered details, on to your towels.

You will need

- high-density sponge, such as upholstery foam
- craft knife and cutting mat
- ruler
- stiff card (stock)
- PVA (white) glue and brush
- pencil
- scissors
- felt-tipped pen
- ceramic paint in various colours
- paint-mixing container
- 15cm/6in square ceramic tiles
- medium artist's paintbrush
- clean cotton cloth
- methylated spirits (methyl alcohol)
- plain light-coloured cotton fabric
- masking tape
- fabric paints
- embroidery hoop
- stranded embroidery thread
- iron
- sewing needle
- dressmaker's pins
- hand towel
- 8 pearl buttons

1 Cut a 15cm/6in square and a 15 × 5cm/6 × 2in rectangle of sponge to make the stamps. Cut a piece of card (stock) for each square and glue one on to each piece of sponge using PVA (white) glue.

2 Scale up the designs at the back of the book to fit a 15cm/6in tile and make paper templates. Draw around the boat, wave and seagull designs on to the square sponge stamp using a felt-tipped pen.

3 Cut away the excess sponge around the design using a craft knife. Repeat on the rectangular sponge to make the second stamp, positioning the waves so that they will fall between the first set of waves.

4 Load the boat stamp with ceramic paints, applying the colours to the different areas using a paintbrush. Clean any grease from the surface of the tiles by rubbing with a cloth dipped in methylated spirits (methyl alcohol). Allow to dry.

6 For the plain wave tiles, re-load the wave stamp with paint and position it 1cm/½in from the bottom edge. Apply the stamp, aligning it with the bottom edge. Print the seagulls at a 45 degree angle above the waves using one, two or three birds to give a varied natural effect.

5 Press the square stamp over the tile. Allow to dry. Load the rectangular waves stamp and stamp another set of waves between the first set. Repeat the boat design on some of the tiles.

7 For the appliqué towel panel, cut out a 17cm/7in square of plain cloth fabric and tape it on to the work surface. Mix fabric paints to match the ceramic paint colours and load the boat stamps as before. Stamp the design on to the fabric and leave to dry.

8 Fix the paints according to the manufacturer's instructions. Insert the panel in an embroidery hoop and work running stitch to pick out the clouds and details on the sail and boat in stranded embroidery thread.

9 Press under a 1cm/½in hem all round the panel and pin it in place at one end of the towel. Work blanket stitch all round the panel to attach it.

10 Stitch a pearl button to each corner of the panel, and one in the middle of each side.

SCANDINAVIAN BEDROOM

This delicate stamped decoration on walls and woodwork is designed to go with the pale colours and painted furniture that characterize period Scandinavian interiors. This is a scheme of great charm, restful on the eye and perfect for a bedroom.

You will need

- matt emulsion (flat latex) paint in grey-blue, off-white and red
- paint-mixing container
- wallpaper paste
- large and medium decorator's paintbrushes
- plumbline
- ruler
- pencil
- high-density sponge, such as upholstery foam
- felt-tipped pen or white crayon
- craft knife
- small paint roller
- fine artist's paintbrush
- matt (flat) acrylic varnish and brush

1 Mix grey-blue emulsion (latex) with 50 per cent wallpaper paste and apply to the walls with a broad paintbrush, working at random angles. Blend the brushstrokes to avoid hard edges.

2 Allow to dry, then repeat the process to soften the effect.

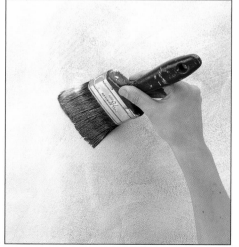

3 Mix off-white emulsion with 75 per cent wallpaper paste. Brush on as before. Allow to dry.

4 Hang a plumbline 2.5cm/1in from one corner and use as a guide to draw a vertical line down the wall.

5 Measure about 40cm/16in across and draw a second vertical line, again using the plumbline as a guide. Repeat all around the room.

6 Trace the template at the back of the book and draw it on a rectangle of high-density sponge using a felt-tipped pen or white crayon. Cut away the excess sponge around the design using a craft knife.

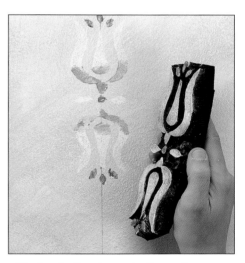

7 Use a small paint roller to load the stamp with off-white emulsion (latex) paint.

8 Add details in red and grey-blue, using a fine artist's paintbrush over the off-white paint.

9 Apply the stamp to the wall, positioning it centrally over the marked line.

10 Repeat, positioning the stamp so that each motif is just touching the preceding one. Work down from the top of the wall.

11 Use the grey-blue wash mixed for the wall base coat to drag the door. Applying pressure to the bristles, pull down in a straight line, following the direction of the wood grain.

12 Apply the paint to the stamp as before, but this time loading only one flower motif. Stamp a single motif diagonally into the corners of each door panel as shown.

13 Add more paint to the grey-blue wash to deepen the colour. Edge the door panels using the artist's paintbrush. Leave to dry, then apply two coats of varnish to the door to protect the design.

ANIMAL FRIEZE

A low frieze is perfect for a nursery as it concentrates interest at the child's own level. Children can't fail to be enchanted by this harmonious troop of animals all sharing the same flowery field, with clouds billowing overhead.

You will need

- emulsion (latex) paint in sky blue, grass green, yellow and white
- paint roller
- large decorator's paintbrush
- fine artist's paintbrush
- paint-mixing container
- stamp inkpads in black, brown and pink
- rubber stamps in cow, chicken, pig and sheep designs
- natural sponge

1 Paint the wall in sky blue emulsion (latex) using a paint roller. Leave to dry.

2 Paint the skirting (base) board in grass green emulsion.

3 Using the same green paint, apply wispy strokes up the wall to create the effect of grass growing up the wall. Allow the paint to dry.

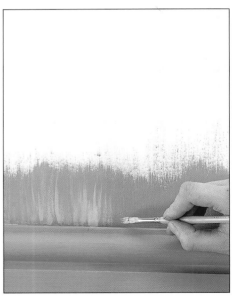

4 Using a fine artist's paintbrush, highlight the grass with a lighter, yellowy green.

5 Paint small daisies in white emulsion at random in the grass. Add yellow centres.

6 Using a black inkpad and rubber stamp, stamp the cow motif randomly along the top of the frieze.

7 Print groups of chickens, using a brown inkpad.

8 Print the pig stamp several times facing the opposite direction, using a pink inkpad.

9 Print the sheep, using black ink. Using the fine paintbrush, fill in the body of the sheep in white emulsion. Do the same with the cows if you wish.

10 Lightly press a natural sponge into white emulsion and sponge cloud shapes on the sky blue wall above the frieze.

STARRY CABINET

Turn a junk-shop find into a unique bedside cabinet using a palette of fresh colours and a simple star motif. Before you start to paint, divide the piece visually into blocks, each of which will be a different colour, with another shade for the frame. Keep all the colours in similar tones to achieve this pretty, sugared-almond effect.

You will need

- medium-grade abrasive paper
- wooden cabinet
- wood filler
- acrylic wood primer
- medium and small decorator's paintbrushes
- emulsion (latex) paint in green, pink, blue and yellow
- wooden knobs
- star rubber stamp
- stamp inkpads in a variety of colours
- drill and drill bit
- screwdriver and screws
- masking tape
- acrylic spray varnish

1 Sand the cabinet to remove any rough patches or old paint or varnish. Fill any holes with wood filler and sand down again. Paint the cabinet with a coat of acrylic wood primer and leave to dry.

2 Paint the cabinet using several different coloured emulsion (latex) paints and allow to dry.

3 Using an assortment of all the colours except that of the frame, paint a row of spots around the edge.

4 Paint the wooden knobs. When the paint has dried, stamp a contrasting star motif on each one using coloured inkpads. When dry, drill screw holes and screw the knobs into position.

5 Stamp a contrasting star motif on to each of the spots around the cabinet frame.

6 Use masking tape to mark out a row of stripes along the bottom of the cabinet and paint them in a contrasting colour, using a fine paintbrush.

7 When all the paint is dry, protect it with a coat of acrylic spray varnish. Leave to dry thoroughly.

TEMPLATES

The templates on the following pages may be re-sized to any scale required. The simplest way of doing this is to enlarge or reduce them on a photocopier. Alternatively, trace the design and draw a grid of evenly spaced squares over your tracing. Draw a larger grid on another piece of paper and copy the outline square by square. Draw over the lines to make sure they are continuous.

HARLEQUIN SCREEN (how to mark the panels and apply the masking tape)
pages 68–71

The pencil marks

The tape marks

FROSTED VASES
pages 99–101

ART NOUVEAU HATBOX
pages 102–4

STAR FRAME
pages 105–7

MAKING
SANDCASTLES
pages 108–11

GREEK URNS
pages 115–17

SEASHORE BATHROOM SET
pages 112–14

FRENCH COUNTRY KITCHEN
pages 122–5

PENNSYLVANIA-
DUTCH TULIPS
pages 118–21

TRAY OF AUTUMN
LEAVES
pages 126–8

HERALDIC DINING
ROOM
pages 154–7

Cut out the darker areas
for the highlight templates

GILDED CANDLES
pages 129–31

RENAISSANCE ART
pages 132–5

GEOMETRIC FLOOR TILES
pages 136–9

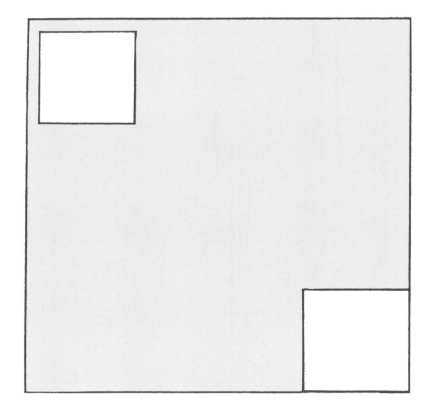

ORGANZA CUSHION
pages 140–2

THROUGH THE GRAPEVINE
pages 146–9

TABLECLOTH AND NAPKINS
pages 143–5

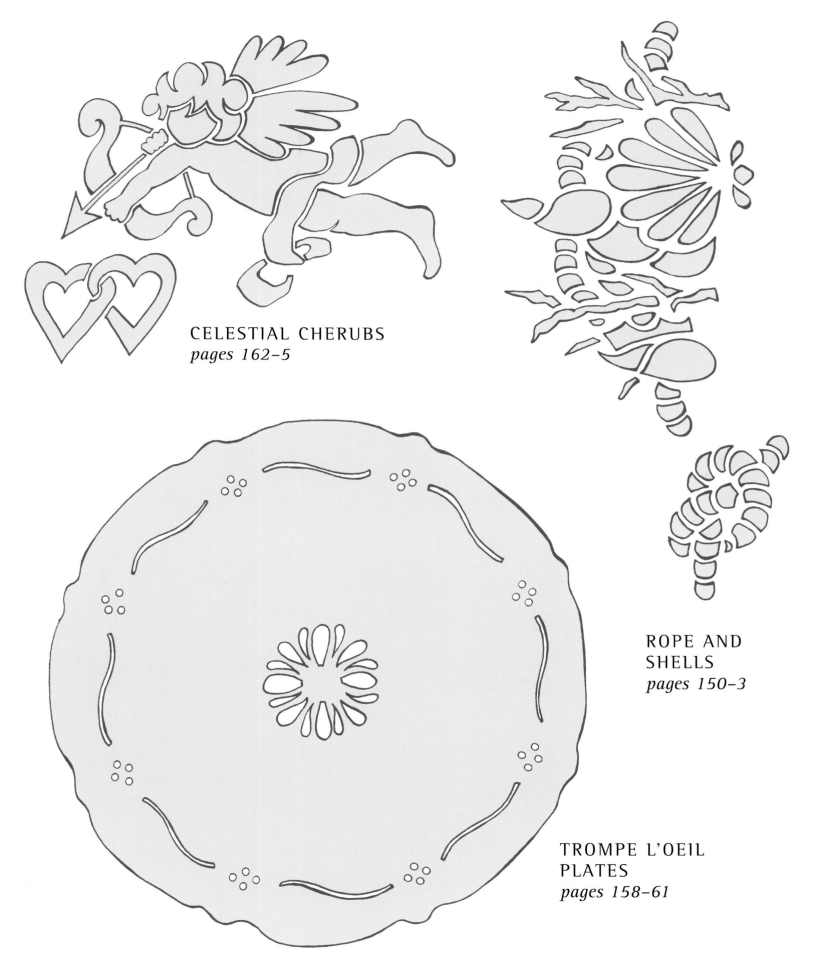

CELESTIAL CHERUBS
pages 162–5

ROPE AND
SHELLS
pages 150–3

TROMPE L'OEIL
PLATES
pages 158–61

GOTHIC DINING ROOM
pages 220–3

SANTA FE LIVING ROOM
pages 202–5

PLASTER WALL TREATMENT
pages 216–19

MOORISH TILE EFFECT
pages 198–201

FOLK-ART CHAIR
pages 206–8

SCANDINAVIAN BEDROOM
pages 230–3

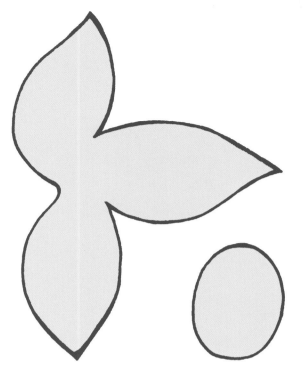

GRAPEVINE FRIEZE AND GLASSES
pages 186–9

STRAWBERRY FRUIT BASKET
pages 179–81

ART NOUVEAU ROSES
pages 212–15

SAILING BOAT
FRIEZE
pages 226–9

INDEX